The Secret Life of a
Weight-Obsessed Woman

The Secret Life of a Weight-Obsessed Woman

Wisdom to Live the Life You Crave

By Iris Ruth Pastor

Portions of this book first appeared as a nine-post blog series at The Huffington Post, 2016.

Cover Design: Robin Brooks, www.TheBeautyofBooks.com
Cover Illustration © Evgladysh / Shutterstock

ISBN (Print) 978-0-9652832-3-6
ISBN (E-book) 978-0-9652832-4-3
Library of Congress Control Number: 2017957116

For a speaker who won't be boring, go off-topic or run on too long, contact irisruthpastor@gmail.com

To sign up for the weekly newsletter, visit www.irisruthpastor.com.

To read Iris's blog, visit irisruthpastor.com/category/blog

Follow Iris on Twitter: @irisruthpastor

And connect with Iris on Facebook, LinkedIn, and Instagram.

Also, for *free* bonus content, visit irisruthpastor.com

Ladies, Ink.
P.O. Box 130443
Tampa Fl 33681

Dedication

Dedicated to my husband,
Steven Allen Pastor, the man in my life
who I always have, and always will, hunger for.
Thank you for giving me the freedom to soar,
the security to fail,
and the love to sustain me
as I do both.

Contents

Part Two: Recovery

Part Three: Re-Engagement

Introduction

I almost died in 2012. By my own hand. Well, actually by my middle three fingers of my right hand. These were the fingers I routinely stuck down my throat to tickle my uvula (more commonly known as "the little thing that hangs in the back of your throat"). I didn't do it for laughs. I tickled it to induce vomiting, in order to rid myself of the mounds of ice cream and other carb-laden goodies I had shoveled in just minutes before.

Today in the United States—the land of plenty—millions of people go to bed each night hungry due to poverty. They simply cannot afford much of the food on supermarket shelves. I am not one of them.

In addition, millions are literally starving themselves to death, victims of a condition known as anorexia nervosa. I am not one of them either.

I have the other eating disorder—bulimia—characterized by repeated cycles of bingeing and purging. Research shows that ED (eating disorder) causes all sorts of threatening conditions. To name just a few: stroke, electrolyte imbalance, rotted teeth, ravaged knuckles, and esophageal cancer.

Celebrities routinely die from ED. Non-celebs, too.

None of these facts about eating disorders was of particular interest to me in 1966, when ED first came courting me. I was a sophomore, out-of-state transfer student attending the University of Florida in Gainesville, unsure of a major field of study. I was 1,000 miles away from my mom and dad for the very first time. My high school boyfriend had just broken up with me.

Along with all the changes I was experiencing at that point in my life, my grounding thought was to stay thin. If I was thin, I could cope. And when I found a way to remain thin and eat all the forbidden stuff I secretly craved—well, I thought I had died and gone to heaven. Little

1

did I know that path could very likely lead me to heaven long before I was due to ascend. Little did I know that my brand of heaven would shortly turn into a hell of my own making.

But that was in the iconoclastic 1960s, way before eating disorders even had a name. Way before campus counseling centers offered treatment. Way before sorority houses would need their plumbing pipes replaced on a regular basis. (Why? Because so many sorority girls were throwing up after binges that their stomach acid was corroding the pipes' interiors.)

ED had found a home and he would reside with me for many years—the one constant in a life of flux. He was a satisfied tenant. I was a very accommodating landlord.

Statistics are not easily forthcoming on the number of baby boomers eating large quantities of food and forcing themselves to throw up after consumption. Jessica Setnick, MS, RD, CEDRD, published an article "Eating Disorders: An Ageless Affliction" on December 28, 2013. She cited the results of studies that "shatter the belief that eating disorders only afflict the young and reveal that boomers have eating disorders at the same rate as teenagers—nearly four percent. And an additional thirteen percent of boomers partake in at least one core eating disorder behavior such as binge eating, self-induced vomiting, excessive exercise or laxative abuse."

At this juncture, there are 76.4 million baby boomers in the United States, according to an April 2014 U.S. Census Bureau report. I know I've got a lot of company—at least 3 million of us.

Leaving a Legacy

I am a voracious reader and have been compulsively buying books—mainly hardbacks—since the age of nineteen. At present I have approximately 2,600 books in my home, proudly and grandly displayed in floor-to-ceiling custom made bookshelves in my living room, family room, loft and guest room. In addition, baskets brimming with even more books grace nearly every nook, cranny and corner of my home. Fiction. Nonfiction. Memoir. Self-help. Biographies. Poetry.

Four out of the 2,600 books I own deal with eating disorders and every single one of them is stashed under my side of the king-size bed I share with my husband. The books' spines are intact. The book covers unopened. The pages unread.

Do you think I am in denial?

In addition, I am also a slice-of-life columnist. I have been writing my "Incidentally, Iris" column since 1989.

I have written about many aspects of my life and my experiences over the years, but the one story I never told—the one topic I never explored nor even obliquely alluded to—was the story of my bulimia: its inception, its persistence, its tenacious grip.

Now is the time.

Why?

There are six good reasons: my six grandchildren. Three girls. Three boys.

The legacy I want to leave my beloved six is not of their Nana hunched over a toilet, vomiting her guts out. Or worse, their Nana found dead in some random ladies' room, drowned in a pool of her own vomit.

No.

The legacy I want to leave is of a woman with a demon who had the courage to stare that demon down, to do what it took to slay the dragon and to emerge to tell her tale.

I fervently hope my coming forth will inspire, motivate and help others who face the same (or different demons) to move toward health, resolution, balance and restoration.

This is My Story

My name is Iris Ruth Pastor and I was bulimic for forty-six years.

I grew up in a Midwestern city in Ohio, the oldest child of three, in an intact family. Welcomed with joy to a World War II veteran and his young bride in 1947, I was loved, doted on, and adored by grandparents, parents and a coterie of cousins and relatives who thought I was just the greatest thing since sliced bread. And I thrived.

I was not sexually abused, beaten, abandoned, betrayed or in any way mistreated. My mom packed my lunches every school day morning and greeted me at the door with a smile when the yellow bus dropped me off at three every afternoon. My dad cemented my swing set into the ground so I could swing as high as I wanted without fear of my entire swing set going airborne. My mom and grandmother packed my closet with the latest schoolgirl fashions—at that time wide, knee-length skirts decorated with felt poodles, propped up with horsehair crinolines. I joined a Brownie group, played after-school kickball with the neighborhood kids and won ribbons in every track meet I entered.

My beloved maternal grandmother died suddenly of pancreatic cancer when I was seven—that may have been when the first crack in my armor appeared. She no longer was there to sew my doll clothes, cut my bangs and feed me mountains of pancakes out on her porch—the porch with the massive striped awning.

My mother soldiered on after the loss, as did I. A new baby came. A new house was purchased. Elementary school ended and seventh grade began, in a brand new, imposing building on a busy corner. Braces were clamped on my teeth and boobs appeared on my chest. Mascara and eyeliner replaced my kickball and Keds. Suddenly I was getting a lot more attention for the way my body looked in a sweater than how it performed at a track meet.

Some young women would unconsciously begin to put on weight to cope with their burgeoning curves and some would diet incessantly to maintain an hourglass structure. Others would starve themselves mercilessly to maintain a waif-like, childlike frame. Me? I began to realize the power my womanly body wielded. And I liked it. And I wanted to find a way to keep it at peak performance. To keep the weight south of 110 pounds. To keep the curves luscious and the cheekbones chiseled. Yet to continue to indulge in those comforting stacks of pancakes.

When was the first time I purged? The first time I went into the bathroom, shut the door, leaned over the commode, stuck my fingers down my throat and threw up everything I had just eaten?

I don't remember.

And where did I even get the idea to purge? I don't quite remember that either. Certainly, in those years—the mid-1960s—the terms bulimia and eating disorder were not household words. Even though dieting was becoming ubiquitous among many females of all ages, many of my peers were also burning their bras, joining hippie communes and turning their back on fashion dictates. I wasn't one of them. I pored over every issue of *Seventeen* magazine and secretly dreamed of being a perky, saucy airline stewardess.

My high school years were spent in trying to control my appetite, and food became a source of angst not comfort. Food no longer fueled my body, enabling it to run like the wind and kick the ball as hard as I could. Food became something to ration, to avoid, to fear. Food led to weight gain. Weight gain led to fat. Fat led to looking ordinary, unremarkable, nondescript. Fatties weren't stewardesses, homecoming queens, cheerleaders or majorettes.

I try to re-create the memory of the first time I threw up what I had eaten and realized I could use that as a means of weight control—that I could eat all my favorite forbidden foods and still maintain a body that served as a male magnet. I'm unable to pin down the exact date. I only know that by the time I had lost my virginity, scored high enough on my SATs to get into an out-of-state university as a transfer student, and was initiated into a sorority, my eating habits were no longer cradled in a cocoon of normalcy. I was bingeing and purging regularly.

This is my story.

Part One: Struggle

Though no one can go back and make a
brand new start, anyone can start from
now and make a brand new ending.
—Carl Bard

The Kid in the Front Row

I didn't start off fat. Measuring twenty-one inches long, I weighed less than six pounds at birth. In fact, my parents frequently reminisced about what a long and skinny baby I was.

Unfortunately, I didn't stay skinny for long. Puberty struck early. In fifth grade, my best friend Faye sported a nineteen-inch waist, on a waif-like frame. I, however, was already twenty-four inches around the middle, five feet in stature, weighing in at a hefty 110 pounds. Much to my chagrin.

Further humiliation occurred in health class, where we were lined up by height and weight. I usually was in the back row, clumped together with the other gangly giants. Pictured here is my fifth grade class from Bond Hill Elementary School. I am the big kid in the front row. (By the way, the love of my life, my husband, Steven, is the little kid in the third row. But that's another story.)

It didn't help that, growing up, kids called me an "over-grown lummox."

Strangely enough, the following is what I found when researching bulimia:

In the dictionary, bulimia is defined as an abnormally voracious appetite; a condition characterized by an unnaturally constant hunger. Bulimia comes from the Greek word boulimia. Bous in Greek means ox. Limos means hunger. Bulimia is also defined as ox-like hunger.

How ironic that my peers unknowingly chose that particular "endearment" as a tool of torment.

At full maturity, I ended up five feet two inches tall, six inches shorter than my husband Steven. Yet I would continue to think of myself as the big kid in the front row. How little did I know then how much that mind-set would define, defile and de-rail me.

I weighed 113 pounds when I got pregnant with my first child. Upon visiting the obstetrician for the first time after the poor rabbit died, I begged him for diet pills. I was terrified of gaining too much weight when pregnant. Looking back, I don't know which was more appalling—me being pregnant in my first trimester and asking for diet pills, or the doctor actually writing me a prescription. I filled the prescription. Good sense prevailed and I never even opened the bottle.

Seeking Solace, Staying Special

When I began bingeing and purging, there was simply no vocabulary to describe what I was doing. At that point, I viewed my strange behavior as not only benign, but as a very fortunate creative by-product of my highly functioning right-brained mind. Once again I had found a clever way to live my life. I could indulge my cravings by bingeing and could control my weight by vomiting. And added to the bliss, when I participated in the binge-purge cycle, my mood seemed to lighten, my angst lessen, and best of all, I remained lean.

And great things happened when the scale was south of 110.

My cheekbones became more prominent.

My love life took off.

My hourglass figure became even more finely chiseled.

I went from ordinary looking to meriting a follow-up once-over.

What eighteen-year-old could resist the allure of that?

I was just one of those unfortunate young women who, when carrying even moderate amounts of excess pounds, disappeared into anonymity. I wasn't one of those "fat girls with a pretty face." As soon as the pounds packed on, my face went from appealing to nondescript. My cheekbones disappeared. My large eyes got scrunchy and my face became bloated and large. And if there was anything I continually craved to be, it was acknowledged, special, and unique. Keeping my weight within reasonable bounds was the key to my outer beauty. My sense of self. My sense of self-worth.

In the fall of my freshman year, I would literally roll out of bed and drag myself to my eight a.m. 19th Century European History class—no makeup, hair ruffled, donning loose-fitting jeans and a rumpled T-shirt pulled from the dirty clothes hamper. And yet, classmates later told me that the graduate student teaching that course had remarked that he found me "provocatively beautiful." By the spring of my freshman year, with fifteen additional pounds packed on my hips, thighs and chin line—no doubt due to late-night pizza orgies—I was the recipient of very few second glances from students, tenured professors or lowly grad assistants. I had become nondescript—blending in among the many. Easily overlooked. Startlingly average. And that I could not tolerate.

I was slavishly addicted to the needle on the scale as my barometer of appeal and worth. It was a teetering, tottering structure on which to attempt to build a life of resoluteness and self-confidence. But, by my sophomore year, with ED by my side, I had a shortcut to self-sufficiency, control, confidence and consistent, enduring attractiveness. As I would slowly learn over the decades that followed, there are very few true shortcuts in life. And shortcuts that are not firmly grounded in self-discipline and positive coping skills only lead to dead ends.

My Beau, ED

At first, going steady with ED felt glamorous and savvy. I could indulge in my food fancies and the pointer on the bathroom scale held steady.

But this relationship soon began to serve a darker purpose, for now I had a safe, non-threatening place to dump my volatile and not-socially-sanctioned feelings—the toilet. Without fear of banishment. Sans criticism. Without disappointing others. Without fear of reprisal.

I was taking control of my tumultuous emotions. I was becoming an exemplary exhibitor of calm and clear-eyed focus. I was actually becoming the go-to girl for friends and family—a safe haven for them to open up and confide in me their woes, fears and indiscretions. Imagine that.

Resisting intense inner scrutiny, I forged forward with ED. I felt safe in the comfort zone I had crafted for myself. ED took care of me. He did what I couldn't do for myself. With ED by my side, I looked to be a highly functioning and competent daughter, wife, mother, friend and slice-of-life columnist. The irony was not lost on me that I signed off each of my weekly columns with the closing, "Keep Coping."

Coping was about all I was able to do. True growth and the freedom to soar were not on the table. My "table" was overloaded with cartons of ice cream, boxes of cake mix, containers of ready-made icing. There was no room for soul searching, introspection or resolute action.

Inside, I was still just a lost, lonely, little girl searching for someone to rescue me.

I would remain in this childlike state, with ED in my hip pocket, for decades. And many years would pass before I allowed myself to see that going steady with ED was more of an affliction than a source of true solace.

No matter how many accolades I received, no matter how many close relationships I fostered, no matter how much I achieved, how much I was admired and how high I reached, ED was indisputable proof that I was weak, undisciplined, lazy, self-destructive and out of control. A complete and utter fraud.

And I had visited too many strange bathrooms to deny the validity of that conclusion.

I saw no way out. No safe portal in the midst of the ever-present storm. I longed for direction. A map to guide me into a safe harbor before my perilous journey ended in a hospital room with a prognosis of death. It seemed that there was no battlefield upon which to wage my war. The war within.

Thank God that on that score I was mistaken.

ED's Stats

He's a tool for anger management.
He's a technique for relaxation.
He's a reward for productivity.

He's a release for overriding tension.

He is also a roaming Don Juan, forever seeking multiple lovers.

Among his conquests are the late Princess Diana of Wales, Margaux Hemingway, Paula Abdul, Terri Schiavo, Jane Fonda, Katie Couric, Cathy Rigby, Jamie-Lynn Sigler, Sally Field, Lindsay Lohan, Elton John, Sharon Osbourne, Gilda Radner, Amy Winehouse, Lady Gaga Joan Rivers, Demi Lovato, Justine Bateman, Britney Spears, Richard Simmons, and Alanis Morissette to name just a few.

ED could be going steady with your senator, mayor, or school superintendent. ED could be going steady with your neighbor, co-worker, boss or friend.

He hails from the land of genetics. (My aunt and other female members of my family have taken him as a steady beau too.)

But that is only his home base. He roams the world—ensnaring and beguiling whoever he can.

He resides comfortably in my head as well as my body. A deficiency in a brain chemical, perhaps?

He is a hard habit to break, even though he clearly is not good for me.

He wreaks bodily havoc: sores in my mouth, scratchy throat, chronic laryngitis, chronic teeth issues, aching back, tight neck and shoulders, heavy chest, persistent cough.

Who cares? I'm in love!

What Constitutes a Binge?

A very close friend, whose daughter suffers with bulimia, asked me how I would describe binge behavior. Here is my reply:

- Eating huge amounts of food in less than two hours, at least two times a week.
- Being unable to stop.
- Zoning out while doing it.

If this is one of the definitions of a bulimic binge, then I have been bulimic since I was nineteen years old. And I am now on the brink of Medicare.

I roughly calculate the decades, years, months, weeks and days I have spent in this state:

4.5 decades
45 years
540 months
2,340 weeks
16,380 days

That is how long I have been bulimic.

And if I spent just one hour every day bingeing and purging, that would add up to just under two years of time spent leaning over, sticking my fingers down my throat and puking up my guts into a toilet bowl.

What else could I have done with that time?

- Completed the first two years of law school
- Learned to speak Spanish fluently
- Attended a ton of yoga classes
- Worked for environmental change
- Mentored a whole slew of students

How I squandered my time.

And if I spent one hour out of every day bingeing and purging and during each binge I ate approximately ten dollars' worth of food, that would add up to $164,000!

I cringe. Is it possible I bought, ate and threw up almost $164,000 worth of food?

What else could I have done with that money?

- Made a substantial down payment on a large house
- Enjoyed a weekly massage for the next forty-four years
- Started a foundation
- Paid law school tuitions
- Set up trust funds for my grandchildren
- Contributed an awful lot of canned goods to the homeless shelter

I squandered my money.

Literally all that time and money down the toilet. It is a hard pill to swallow.

A Lover Hovers as Chaos Comes Calling

There is a period of time—two years to be exact—that I do manage to leave my lover, ED.

It happens suddenly. Or so it seems. One day I notice that the urge to binge and purge has decreased. Then I notice that the urge to binge and purge has greatly decreased. Then I notice the urge to binge and purge has ceased altogether.

How can this be?

I take stock.

I seem to be living my dream existence. I am married to a man who appears to be as strong inwardly as his highly muscled outward physique depicts. I am married to a man who, occupationally, is enjoying "rookie of the year" status. And, after looking at over 128 vacant houses, we have just moved into "the perfect one." And while I was away traveling with the kids, my husband bought me the car I secretly had coveted for years. All this makes me feel secure, cherished and well taken care of. But am I?

I begin to bloom in that rich, loamy atmosphere. I start writing my slice-of-life column that to this day is still being published. I begin a children's parenting magazine that would later be merged with a larger publication and would provide the experience and expertise I needed to later become the editor of a weekly newspaper in my hometown.

But, little did I know how illusory my idyllic existence would prove to be. And how very short-lived.

Soon I would be faced with a husband who needed my input, support and direction.

Soon I would be faced with dwindling financial resources incapable of sustaining our lifestyle.

Soon I would be faced with assuming leadership of a family in need of a rudder.

Soon I would be faced with countless decisions on how to productively move my family positively forward.

The Gorilla in the Living Room

ED's been gone two years.

It's two a.m. I am sitting in my burled-wood-paneled study, on the first floor of my grand new home, located in an upscale neighborhood in my hometown. I am surrounded by original art purchased from a nearby gallery. The darkness of the night is shut out by my decorator-designed, custom-made shades with ostentatious pulls adorning each window. The feeling of safety is illusory.

I don't notice the accoutrements, nor bask in the blessed solitude and quiet. I am hunched over a ledger, deep in thought. I am no accountant, but night after night I have been poring over figures. And night after night, I am drawing the same conclusion: our expenses are outpacing our income. We have over-improved our home and, in approximately six months, we will have exhausted our savings. We cannot afford to maintain our current lifestyle. To add to this untenable situation, my self-employed husband has a bad back, which is acting up—preventing him from going to work and making a living.

At lunchtime the following day, I am sitting in a bagel shop, accompanied by my five-year-old son. He is eagerly gobbling up his pizza bagel before we head downtown to watch the Cincinnati Reds trounce their archrival, the St. Louis Cardinals. As I pay the check, a crashing wave of fear washes over me as I recall our dire situation. The call for definitive action is glaringly apparent. I need time to devise and develop a plan of options and actions aimed at alleviating the emotional angst, the monetary bleeding and my husband's health crisis. I need to step up to the plate on our own family's playing field.

Besieged with anxiety, the thought of leisurely taking in a baseball game becomes repulsive to me. Heedless of my son's anguished pleas not to change our plans, I plead an excruciating migraine and head for home. I make only one stop: at the dairy for a gallon of caramel rippled vanilla ice cream.

ED's back in town.

And So It Goes

With time, the crises are resolved. We sell our dream home and move to a more modest one. My husband goes through major back surgery and rehabilitation and then returns to work. We adapt and soldier on. Our family remains intact.

Unfortunately, my initial experience of shedding ED during calm interludes was never to be repeated. ED once again takes up permanent residence. Years pass—soul-searching years, but not action years. It's no wonder. There are perks to staying in denial:

ED's a safety net for my angst.

ED keeps me coping and I am a champion at that.

ED allows me to eat "all the good stuff" I want without my hips widening and my Sophia Loren look-alike cheekbones disappearing.

Slowly, however, the desire to be the captain of my own ship begins creeping into my consciousness. I am tired of ED sabotaging my hours of evening solitude. After my husband goes to bed each night, I long for the ability to veg out comfortably with a good book, delve into a knitting project or simply suffuse myself in the ambience that living in comfortable, familiar surroundings brings. I am so tired of fighting with myself as the evening hour approaches over whether I will or will not keep company with ED. I am resentful of his heavy harness incessantly pulling me back into his harmful lair.

What is the downside of maintaining the status quo?

What is the downside of continuing to binge and purge?

- Guilt
- Remorse
- Encroachingly apparent adverse physical symptoms
- Continued loss of control over my own destiny and life
- Vastly disappointed psyche
- Pessimism and fear for the future

The price was getting too steep.

Tweetily Dee, Tweetily Dum

I am like most people who like to talk and hear themselves talk. I talk about things too much, too often and with too little thought—except when it comes to my real problem: bulimia and its tenacious hold. On that topic, my tongue is tied. Was my bulimia a personal weakness? A disease? A condition? An addiction? A disorder? A character flaw? A bad habit?

I go round and round and round in circles, trying to parse out the truth.

I am consumed by desperate efforts to rid myself of ED. My habitual mantra of "It will be better tomorrow. Tomorrow I will try harder" proves heartbreakingly ineffective. I continually try to stop, yet my trying leads to an increase of bingeing and purging, which leads to increased desperation and despair. My self-image is tarnished, altered, irretrievably damaged. Many moons have waxed and waned since I viewed myself as someone who could overcome obstacles. The flames of failure engulf me.

No triumphs grace my doorsteps. My attempts to eat normally are short-lived. Botched. Diminishing. My spiritual flame burns low, sizzles almost to extinction—like a flickering candle petering out with still so much wick unused.

Comfort is found anonymously—on Twitter—provided by others tormented like me.

Here are some of their tweets:

> *If I can't see my bones, I'm nothing.*
> *I long for that feeling to not feel at all. I need saving from myself.*
> *My family thinks I'm an alien from planet depressed.*
> *Be skinny or die trying.*
> *This year is going to be different she says every year.*
> *I miss the person I once was.*
> *I want to be thin more than anything, and if I die getting there, so be it.*
> *I wanna hear about the inner workings of one of those pretty girls who seem to get whatever she wants.*
> *I puke, therefore I feel.*
> *Just another girl fighting for perfection.*

Welcome to the dark side.

The Guru of Coping

"The Guru of Coping" is how I appeared to the world. Coping and appeared are key words in that statement.

My mom and my dad both often remarked that I was the glue that held everyone together. I arbitrated. I smiled. I hugged them. My younger sister knew she could rely on me to handle everything calmly and with a sense of humor. I basked in her opinion of my competence.

Cousins relied on me to tell their daughters things they wouldn't listen to if it came from their own mothers' mouths: Don't drink excessively on Friday nights. Wear your retainer. Dial it down with the exposed cleavage.

Young mothers looked up to me to advise them on how to balance it all: misbehaving kids, bored husbands, stalled careers, untidy family rooms.

Faithful readers of my weekly slice-of-life column wrote me letters filled with admiration and support for my observations on daily living.

Professional groups and associations clamored to hear my inspirational and motivational talks on being the best you can be.

People adrift noted the closing signature of my column was "Keep Coping" and readily assumed I was following my own admonition.

During the years I broadcasted a Sunday night radio show, radio station personnel marveled at my on-air and off-air equanimity—questioning my husband whether I was always so upbeat and energetic. My husband answered yes. I got his discretion, but wondered if he really bought into the facade I was always so carefully cultivating. Surely he knew something was amiss if I had to continue to binge and purge in order to cope. Didn't he realize what I was really doing after he went to bed each night?

I kept my questions to myself and he didn't push to get closer to the truth. And when he would intermittently and regularly ask me if anything was wrong, I would emphatically answer that everything was "peachy keen." Did I look him in the eyes when I replied? Did I exude sarcasm? And if I did, did he pick up what I was subliminally pitching? I don't know.

My mantra was and continued to be: "Self-Preservation Trumps Intimacy."

Feeling Like a Fraud

I always felt like such a fraud. On the surface, I appeared serene, confident, in control and exuding vitality. Underneath, I was not what I appeared to be. I was nervous, agitated, unhappy and lacking self-assurance. Forces I could neither understand nor control were driving me relentlessly to binge and purge daily. That was not the arbiter of a mature, well-balanced and highly functioning adult. It was all such a pitiful façade.

Highly aware of the corrosive stomach juices spilling over my teeth nightly during my purges, I also focused on maintaining the best dental hygiene I could—visiting my dentist every three to four months for cleanings. And root canals. And crowns. And caps. And mouth guards. And dental implants. Wisdom teeth extractions. Dry sockets. Since I lived in a few different cities over those years, I recall seeing at least four different dentists as a regular patient. Not one of them ever mentioned to me that they suspected an eating disorder was at the root (pun intended) of my dental problems.

In my bulimic years, I saw many doctors for minor health issues and routine checkups. I never confided in them about my bulimia and if they suspected anything was amiss, they kept it to themselves. After all, I was Miss Coper. Miss Do-It-All Perfectly. Letting a professional close enough to pierce my fragile armor was not in my bag of tricks. And besides, because most of these guys and their wives ran in our social circle, I did not regard them as safe havens.

Only one doctor in all those forty-six years of my bingeing and purging came close to picking up ED's presence. He was a young South African internist, trained in Western medicine, and as he jokingly referred to it, "voodoo" medicine (integrative medicine). Upon examining me on my initial visit, he pronounced I had agitation emanating from my stomach.

No shit.

I remained unresponsive and tight-lipped. The exam continued uninterrupted.

Mental Mini-Breaks

Searching for the funny, amusing and wry diminishes the anguish over my binge-purge habit.

I pour my energies into developing a sense of humor. I read the comics daily. It helps me weather the instability of the days and adapt more readily to the healthy changes in routine I am attempting to make. Often I find myself running off five copies of the same joke and sending each one to my sons—an attempt to keep connected. And I search the Internet for meaningful quotes—a benign, safe way to keep grounded and occupied as I experience the silent upheaval of my days.

Here are some of my favorite short quips:

If you must choose between two evils, pick the one you've never tried before.

My idea of housework is to sweep the room with a glance.

Age is a very high price to pay for maturity.

A closed mouth gathers no feet.

Always yield to temptation, because it may not pass your way again.

Bills travel through the mail at twice the speed of checks.

Men are from Earth. Women are from Earth. Deal with it.

A balanced diet is a cookie in each hand.

Middle age is when broadness of the mind and narrowness of the waist change places.

Junk is something you throw away three weeks before you need it.

By the time you can make ends meet, they move the ends.

Thou shalt not weigh more than thy refrigerator.

Blessed are they who can laugh at themselves for they shall never cease to be amused.

And some longer vignettes:

The Garden of Eden

One day in the Garden of Eden, Eve calls out to God, "Lord, I have a problem!"

"What's the problem, Eve?"

"Lord, I know you created me and provided this beautiful garden and all of these wonderful animals and that hilarious snake, but I'm just not happy."

"Why is that, Eve?" came the reply from above.

"Lord, I am lonely, and I'm sick to death of apples."

"Well, Eve, in that case, I have a solution. I shall create a man for you."

"What's a man, Lord?"

"A man is a flawed creature, with many flawed character traits. He'll be stubborn, vainglorious, and self-absorbed. All in all, he'll probably give you a hard time. But…he'll be bigger, faster and will revel in childish things like fighting and kicking a ball about. He won't be too smart, so he'll also need your advice to think properly."

"Sounds great," says Eve, with an ironically raised eyebrow. "But what's the catch, Lord?"

"Well… you can have him on one condition."

"What's that, Lord?" Eve asks.

"As I said, he'll be proud, arrogant and self-admiring…so you'll have to let him believe that I made him first. Just remember, it's our little secret…you know, woman to woman."

The Saga of the Little Bird

Once there was a little bird that decided to stay in the north for the winter. However, it soon turned so cold that he reluctantly started to fly south.

Ice began to form on his wings. Almost frozen, he fell to earth in a pasture. A cow wandered over and—excuse the verb—pooped on the little bird. Our feathered friend thought it was the end.

But the manure was warm and defrosted his wings. Comfortable, happy and able to breathe, he started to sing. Just then, a cat came by and hearing the chirping, investigated. The cat cleared away the manure, found the singing bird and promptly ate him.

The moral of the story is:

Anyone who dumps a little brown present on you is not necessarily your enemy.

Anyone who pulls you out a pile of manure is not necessarily your friend.

And, if you're warm and happy in that pile, keep your mouth shut!

Vacationing Without ED

For my husband and me, who were raising five kids, vacations were sporadic and irregular. Something we held sacred. Prized highly. Eagerly anticipated. This was because there always seemed to be a pressing need to divert funds elsewhere—orthodontists, soccer equipment, summer camp, tutoring, bar mitzvah savings accounts. So we took very few vacations, even though the majority of us had a wanderlust spirit, thrived on adventure and craved seeking out places we had never been. When we did vacation, much to his chagrin, I left ED at home, sulking. There was simply no room in my suitcase for ED, though he did try to sneak in a few times while I was packing.

Getting away from the stressors of daily life helped me leave ED behind.

The change of scenery eased my dependence on him.

Taking my meals with others protected me.

Being relaxed and happy in an unfamiliar environment shielded me. Lack of privacy added to my armor, I must admit.

What I remember most vividly about ED when it comes to vacations is how joyously he welcomed me home. And how glad I was to see him, too.

Cultivating a Cushioned Atmosphere

Maya Angelou has a famous quote on the subject of what you're supposed to do when you don't like something:

"What you're supposed to do when you don't like a thing is change it. If you can't change it, change the way you think about it. Don't complain."

Well, I certainly didn't complain about my bulimia. Who would I complain to? It was a secret to all but a few people.

And, yes, it was within my control to stop bingeing and purging, as it was of my own making. But why would I change things? It served a purpose: it kept me coping. And coping was my watchword.

So I fervently believed not only that I wouldn't change, but that I couldn't change—because as hard as I tried to break off with ED, he kept reappearing. So I took Maya's advice and changed how I thought about ED.

Instead of looking at my bulimic condition as a self-destructive vice that kept me emotionally stuck, that kept in me in disequilibrium, that kept me isolated and depressed, I changed how I thought about it. I simply regarded ED as a bad habit, a difficult-to-break bad habit—something I had to endure and contain. So I put ED in a silo, rode the wave when he appeared, and then stowed him back in his neat and tidy corner. Where I hoped he would stay put.

Hoping is not a plan.

Eroding the Mission

Another quote from Maya Angelou impacts me, but again, perhaps not quite in the way she intended.

"I've learned that people will forget what you said, people will forget what you did, but people will never forget how you made them feel."

I like to think I did a good job at making each person I encountered feel good about himself, but I failed abysmally at doing what it took to make myself feel good about me.

Shining a Light Down the Rabbit Hole

I am beginning to realize I eat more when I am tired.

And I know where eating more leads.

Secret Shedding

Sometime during our second decade of marriage, I shared my shameful secret with Steven. I could tell he couldn't really understand. He thought I threw up because I was nauseous. He thought I could just stop. He clearly didn't know ED.

Maybe in the ensuing days Steven researched bulimia and learned more about its insidious influence. I don't really know. At my insistence, we didn't talk much about it. But we did develop over the years an unwritten agreement: Coming downstairs after retiring early to bed each evening was off-limits for him; preparing for and executing my binges and purges were something I did in solitude.

Reckoning

ED and I started "dating" in 1966. Forty-six years later, we were still together. On Valentine's Day 2012, I hit a new low and simply knew I could no longer go on the way I was going. I could not keep doing this to myself. This destructive relationship with ED had to be terminated.

I began to reckon with and confront reality:

I have a loving immediate family and extended family.

I have been married to my husband, Steven, for thirty-six years and hope we will be blessed with many more years together. I know that he will never forgive me if, by intentionally harming myself, I shorten my own life.

Among other things, I have been:
- A slice-of-life columnist
- The editor of a weekly Jewish newspaper
- A motivational speaker
- A radio talk show host
- An author, with my mom, of *Slices, Bites and Other Facts of Life*
- And a pretty involved daughter, wife, mother, sister, co-worker and friend

Reality prompted me to begin thinking about the legacy I will leave my family.

Taking Action

A recognition of past teeny, tiny mouse steps I have taken that have resulted in accomplishment and empowerment in other areas of my life start bleeding into my sick relationship with ED. If I can confront a co-worker, if I can be honest with a good friend, if I can master the art of cold calling, if I can confidently accept the managing editor position of a weekly newspaper, if I can talk openly with a child over a disappointment, if I can launch and sustain a motivational speaking career—then, perhaps, I am stronger than I think. Perhaps breaking free of ED is a real possibility too.

I start tentatively thinking about what I can do to jumpstart the process. To make a few small changes.

One afternoon, late in the day, I find myself searching the Internet for a psychologist who specifically treats eating disorders. I find one and make an appointment.

I am nervous as I sit before her for the first time, the words sticking in my mouth as I confess my dirty, dark and shameful secret. I sheepishly remark that, after forty-six years, I am probably the longest surviving bulimic on record. She doesn't respond.

She seems nonplussed, unaware of what a benchmark moment this contrite act of confession is for me. She seems unimpressed by the staunch bravery I feel I am exhibiting, just by showing up and opening up. She seems unaware that my insides are coated with a layer of oily, sheer terror.

I give our sessions a few more tries and break my fourth appointment. I never return.

Months pass.

After a particularly violent bout of bingeing and purging, I go back to desultorily searching the web and, lo and behold, an entry pops up that I have never seen before—a substance abuse and eating disorder rehab center located about an hour from my home. I eagerly peruse their website, immediately drawn to the information on their outpatient treatment program.

Once more I am filled with hope and make an appointment with the head psychiatrist.

I like her immediately, even though in retrospect, it is for the most superficial of reasons: her unruly hair that refuses to be coaxed into a contrived hairdo. Her funky, clunky jewelry. Her bohemian clothes. And her engaging smile.

I begin to talk. And she listens.

I admit to her that bulimia was taking a toll. My chest ached upon the mildest exertion. My neck had limited mobility. My throat was constantly sore and my voice hoarse. And as I was wont to admit, I was fast coming to terms with the fact that I couldn't kick ED out without back-up help. Lord knows I had tried.

I tell her that I am fearful. Desperate and discombobulated. I do not know if I am up to the challenge of staring down and slaying my long-enduring, persistent, consistent beau. My mood alternates between wild bouts of despair and hopelessness, to euphoric waves of optimism and free-ranging joy.

I commit to beginning treatment shortly after Valentine's Day.

And I keep my hands over my ears so I can block out ED's voice screaming, "Bad Move. Bad Move. Bad Move." Its echo would follow me for days.

Leaving My Lover

Though she is willing for me to try a three-day-per-week outpatient treatment program, the psychiatrist doubts that after so many years of going steady with ED that I will be able to break-up with him without in-patient care. That observation stops me cold. Not only is that reality horrifying to me, it is simply not doable given my family situation. How do I just disappear without anyone knowing the truth? Like my parents, my five children, my siblings and close friends? And I am not ready to spill the beans—at least not until I have experienced a modicum of success. And who knows if that will ever happen? Better to keep my struggle under wraps for now.

And I have a full-time job.

No, residential treatment for me is simply not a viable option. I feel comfortable with the idea of working out the kinks in my wrinkled body and mind while returning to my own bed and my own routine after each weekday session.

But I know the clouds of change are gathering. The daily onslaught of guilt and remorse that washes over me every time I stick my fingers down my throat to throw up have finally outweighed and overruled the benefits of staying with ED. He is an adolescent crush that needs shredding and shedding. He has long outlasted his usefulness.

And the winds of reckoning are starting to gain momentum too. Once unleashed into a powerful tailwind, the gale's force cannot be deflected by ED's faux power. For the first time in a long time, I want to believe in myself and take back my power. Most significantly, I want to be on the inside what I have for so long appeared to be on the outside: healthy, in control and charting my own course.

I vow to carry that warrior-like demeanor into treatment. I will need it.

My Last Binge

My last binge started and ended with little drama.

It was February 14, 2012—another Valentine's Day when I felt rather despondent because the loving accolades I yearned for hadn't materialized.

I was in the half bath, downstairs, with the door locked.

My husband was asleep upstairs. The television was set to CNN, with the volume low so as not to wake my husband. I had just finished throwing up a half gallon of chocolate chip cookie dough ice cream and was already beginning to wonder what else I could eat and vomit up before climbing the stairs to bed.

As I flushed the last of the ice cream down the toilet, I happened to catch a glance of my face in the oversized vanity mirror. Horrified, I stared at the unfamiliar image. My skin was blotchy, my eyes—always my best feature—were bloodshot and teary. My chin sported a glop of something half-digested from dinner that I had no interest in further investigating.

"This is how you want your grandchildren to see you?" I asked myself miserably. "A crazed wreck of a woman?"

Slowly I made my way to the door, turned the handle and walked out into the dimly lit, cooler hallway.

Right then and there, I vowed that never, ever again would I vomit after a food binge. Strangely enough, it was a humbling, no-big-deal moment.

There was no band playing. No eager loving friends and family cheering me as I crossed the finish line on my self-destructive path. No backslaps, no hearty voices of encouragement. Just a quiet family room, a TV and me. I was alone, but strangely, not terrified.

I finally found the courage to utter the words I never quite could say before: "ED, it's over."

Instantly, I felt rudderless. Frightened. Disoriented and alone. But I also felt hopeful. Optimistic. Buoyant. I took a deep breath. I squared my shoulders. I reached out for help and support to beat ED to a pulp and silence his beckoning call.

Six months before my sixty-fifth birthday—poised on the brink of Medicare—I decided I wanted to both grow up and own up. I wanted to be a woman. I wanted to be the best I could be. Not perfect. But good enough.

And so began my journey to resolution and re-engagement.

Poof

Just a few days later my new-found resolve is tested. My son is taking the Florida bar exam today and tomorrow. I realized that he had not studied last night and was still sleeping this morning and could possibly be late for his exam.

My husband said I was over-reacting. My husband said that relaxing the night before a large exam was a sound idea. My husband said that our son had plenty of time this morning to get to the testing place.

My husband's logical assessment of the situation drove me crazy. My super lunacy probably did the same to him.

Recognizing that the unwarranted fury building up inside me was probably somewhat misplaced, I consciously drove my anger in a different direction—not inward, but outward. I started doing my stair exercises, the ones I usually do at night. And as I climbed and descended the twisting front hall stairwell again and again, I diverted my thoughts to more productive and pleasurable pursuits: fine tuning details for an upcoming luncheon event I was planning for work and visualizing the walls in my living room painted in fat stripes of bold color.

I couldn't control the outcome of the bar exam, but I could control my anxiety over my son taking the two-day test. And so what normally would have been a trigger for a binge and purge went poof.

Part Two: Recovery

Success is the sum of small efforts,
repeated day in and day out.
—Robert Collier

Authenticity

I am beginning to understand my own authenticity. Quite simply, I am getting what I am all about. I feel like, somehow along the way, I lost my sense of sacred obligation to myself. I lost the courage and fortitude to hone my unique talents.

I am an author, a columnist, a storyteller. A seeker of wisdom and a purveyor of information. I have been afforded the opportunity to receive professional treatment for my eating disorder. I must not squander this privilege. I am propelled to shine up my rusty writing skills, to fully utilize my newly minted powers of introspection and wisely begin the process of telling my tale.

It's a story rife with despair, riddled with hopelessness. But, it is also a healing story of a bulimic's battle to honestly explore her motives, her behavior and the consequences of her actions—in order to be free of her demons. And we all have demons—these demons that we endeavor to hide because of fear and shame and guilt. Mine involved flushing the not-neat, the not-tidy, and the not-socially-acceptable feelings I harbored down the toilet through vomiting. Others cope by soaking in alcohol excess or shooting up with drugs. Or cutting. Or shoplifting. Or a million other self-destructive acts.

Jennifer Nospartak, a student at the University of Michigan Graduate School of Social Work, talks about the notion of *Tikkun Olam*, "repairing the world through human actions."

Humanity's responsibility to change, improve, and fix its earthly surroundings is powerful, she says. It implies that each person has a hand in working towards the betterment of his or her own existence, as well as the lives of future generations.

I am a Reform Jew who holds the concept of *Tikkun Olam* close to my heart.

I understand that *Tikkun Olam* forces people to take ownership of their world in an effort to bring the world back to its original state of holiness.

Change one person and you change the world.

I'm on it.

I want to tell my story. I want to spread my story. Too many fellow sufferers feel what I feel, but may not or cannot put those feelings into words. In laying bare my story, I hope to do my small part to dissipate the darkness surrounding eating disorders. To help fellow sufferers emerge into the light.

I am growing, transforming, fertilizing, cultivating and preserving my bloom.

This flower has a story to tell.

My Story Continues

Shortly after I transferred to the University of Florida my sophomore year, I started dating a cute guy I met at a pre-football tailgating party. All my sorority sisters squealed with rage the first time he stepped into the AEPhi house in the fall of 1966.

"Where's he been hiding?" they all begged to know.

"In plain sight," I replied airily, as he whisked me out the door and escorted me to his navy blue and white GTO convertible.

I married him a year later—not because I was madly in love. I wasn't. Not because I was pregnant. I wasn't. I married him because I perceived he was safe, strong and secure. I married him because I thought he could save me from myself. I married him because I thought he had the power to steer me into calm waters, to still the uncertainty of my life's direction. To stop me from the poor choices I was making.

The young man I picked to marry was good-looking, kind and attentive. Unfortunately, that wasn't enough for me. I wanted someone who would take care of me forever so I didn't have to. I wanted someone who could solve my problems so I didn't have to.

Fairy tale endings only happen in fairy tales. Real life is grittier. Real life demands we face our own shortcomings and seek solutions to our issues. Not surprisingly, Gary and I divorced seven years later. Our crowning achievement: two sons who would give us much joy in the coming years. Our most enduring triumph: emerging from a fractured marriage devoid of rancor and visions of revenge—and forging a friendship based on trust and deep affection.

I took my divorce decree and my two boys and headed back home to Ohio. And then, a serendipitous event would alter my life forever. I met my true love at our tenth high school reunion. I married Steven a year later and proceeded to give birth to three more boys in rapid succession.

Change of scene. Change of heart. Change of partner. Change of name. Change of family configuration. But one thing didn't change. ED was still hanging around.

To Be or Not to Be Committed

It's been a few weeks now since my last binge and, paradoxically, since signing the papers to seek outpatient treatment, I have not had the urge to binge and purge. Hey, maybe I was over-reacting. Hey, maybe I don't really need such drastic action in order to stop the binge/purge cycle of abuse.

Momentarily, I think about canceling my outpatient treatment contract altogether—about saving the time and money.

Perhaps I should explore a less invasive course of action, such as an online treatment program?

Just earlier today I found a website for bulimics which provided great insights. Deprivation leads to bingeing. And no matter how much you purge, calories still linger in your digestive tract, which is why bulimics are not "skinny bitches." Maybe reading websites is all I need.

Or I could just continue as I had been, slugging through alone?

My gut tells me to stay the course with the three-day-per-week outpatient treatment program. Face-to-face contact is necessary for me to succeed. As is a measure of structure. And accountability.

I reluctantly recognize that a connection exists between committing to treatment and being on my best behavior. I know that I lack the courage to seek help when in an out-of-control state. I prefer to be in a state of "relative" equilibrium when I begin baring my soul.

And it's already working. Since committing to treatment, but not yet actually starting, I've experienced an energy surge. Tired of being taken of advantage of, I went to my supervisor at work to discuss my paltry wages. And I informed the editor of the small paper I write for that there will be no more columns until I am paid in full.

I think I am beginning to like Iris.

Temporarily Breaking Free of the Clutch

The night before starting treatment, I experience a perfect storm of events. I go out for dinner with some girlfriends. I dive (not literally) into a giant bowl of crispy, well-oiled French fries. I come home to a quiet house—my husband upstairs, already fast asleep. I plan on watching the Academy Awards and at the commercial breaks, employing my usual self-destructive ritual of getting rid of the large quantity of food I had previously eaten. The reality that I would be beginning treatment the following afternoon keeps me glued to the couch during commercials instead of purposively heading to the bathroom to throw up.

"How long," I wonder, "will the novelty of being in treatment keep me free of ED's clutches?"

I will soon find out.

At First...

My outpatient treatment at Fairwinds begins. I am part of a group comprised of both men and women. The youngest is fifteen, driven to the treatment center after school by her mom, in a blue station wagon. I am the oldest. I leave work early three days a week and drive myself to the center. Each time, I listen to classical music as I barrel down the highway and over the bridge, but the transition from a respected professional to a vulnerable patient remains jarring.

I soldier on, resisting the urge to mother and hover over the younger members.

I tell them I think I look normal.

I function, rising each day to fulfill my responsibilities.

I appear healthy, well adjusted, relatively sane and in control.

Participatory. Attractive. Engaged.

And why do I think I appear so normal?

Because I have a secret weapon in my arsenal: ED.

I tell them that he is in my corner.

He is my go-to guy.

He is my compass.

My very own navigation system.

My master.

My mate.

He reigns supreme when I am:
- Happy
- Frustrated
- Satisfied
- Disappointed
- Fulfilled
- Hungry
- Rested

- Tired
- Lonely
- Surrounded by others
- Anxious
- Calm
- Not measuring up
- Exceeding all expectations

I tell them that ED is so damn easygoing. He asks nothing in return for his constant companionship, except loyalty and dedication to the core mission: live a lie and continue to hurt myself.

ED is the treat I allow myself at the end of the day for getting through the day with a modicum of grace and dignity, for coping—even at times excelling—and tending to others.

He sustains me.

But ED is also my nemesis—the one who, deep down, makes me feel like a fraud, a phony, a pitiful mess.

Silence reigns when I complete my litany. I think the group is stunned by my artful articulation of my situation and puzzled why my insights don't trump my destructive actions.

I am too.

The Group

I had many hesitations about beginning treatment at an eating disorder center. Participating in group therapy sessions was one of them, centering on anonymity and age.

At present I live in Tampa, but I did not grow up here. Therefore, I seldom run into high school, elementary school or even preschool cronies. So, when seeking outpatient programs at eating disorder treatment centers, I felt pretty assured of anonymity when I stumbled upon Fairwinds, located in an abutting county.

How wrong I would prove to be.

Hesitation about the demographic makeup of the group was also a concern. At age sixty-four, I didn't want to be in a therapy group with a bunch of teenagers. I felt I was light years beyond their high school angst. I longed to be paired with women who had been battling ED for years—maybe even decades—and were intent on eradicating him.

How faulty that assumption would prove to be too. Ironically, I would learn a great deal about my fifteen-year-old self during group therapy from the sprinkling of budding adolescents and teenage girls in our group.

I walk into the outpatient therapy group at Fairwinds for the very first time, conflicting thoughts and emotions swirling furiously around in my head. The first thing that registers is that there are six people there—five females and one male.

"Okay, I can live with one male," I reckon. "He will perhaps offer a different perspective to the group."

The second thing that registers is that not all five women are below voting age.

"Okay," I note gleefully. "I can live with that too, although clearly one is not even eligible to drive."

The third thing that registers is that one of them at first blush seems to be around my age.

"Even better," I surmise.

The fourth thing that registers is that, upon closer scrutiny, the older woman looks vaguely familiar. Actually, more than vaguely familiar. I know this woman personally. She looks at me. I look at her. And we both gasp in disbelief.

She is a friend I met at a journalism conference in Boston years ago, long before I had even contemplated moving to Florida.

The serendipitous turn of events doesn't end there. Upon meeting her initially, I had learned that her husband hailed from the same small suburb of Cincinnati that I was then living in, our mothers shared the same first and last name, and we shared the same profession: writing.

Upon relocating to Tampa, I had looked her up and we met for dinner. What was memorable about our meal was that she confessed to me that she was a life-long anorexic. I recall serenely listening to her tale of anguish, clucking sympathetically at all the appropriate places, while eating in a normal manner. However, hours later, as soon as my key opened the door to my house, I headed straight for the commode and promptly vomited up my entire meal—along with my great angst over hearing her tale, and my guilt over not sharing mine.

"Oh my God!" we both exclaimed at the same moment. "We know each other," we screeched.

"I hope this isn't a problem," the therapist interrupted. We both assured her it would not be, but I wasn't totally convinced. I was picking up on a degree of hostility emanating from her waif-like frame—centered, I was sure, on my failure to confess to her my own eating issues at our lengthy dinner.

I didn't have long to wait until my vague feeling was confirmed.

"I knew you had an eating disorder the first time we met years ago at that conference," she testily announced. "I could tell by your food choices and portions."

"Really," I shot back, "I always thought I hid it pretty well."

I would like to say that she and I re-connected mightily during our group therapy sessions. That didn't happen. She was at a very critical juncture in her life: divorced from her husband, out of work and seemingly still in the clutches of her eating disorder. She scared me. When she confessed that a trip for pleasure caused such great anxiety over the food she would be eating while away that she seriously contemplated canceling her trip, I knew that she was what I feared I could turn into. I had a supportive husband, a satisfying job, and so far had resisted the impulse to allow my eating disorder to interfere with every aspect of my social life—be it traveling, going out to dinner with friends or attending parties.

Ironically, as I was to learn through multiple group sessions, the gripping hold ED exercised over me was just as entrenched as its hold over her. She just recognized its presence. I was clueless.

46

I began to see through the group members' observations just how my bulimia manifested itself intermittently throughout my day—throughout my life. Counting calories. Anxiously peering into any available mirror to check on the prominence of my cheekbones. Feeling depressed about my body. Feeling guilt over my lack of self-control. Feeling bad about my inability to stick to a diet and successfully reach and maintain my ideal weight. Mad at myself because I could not stop bingeing and purging every chance I got.

Like my friend, how many wasted hours of creative thought were flushed down the toilet—pushed out of the way—by repetitive, mind-numbing, self-defeating thought patterns and actions centered on food, weight, and eating?

My guess? Quite a few—for both of us.

My Dream

Dreams abound during the course of my therapy. I have a dream, but I know not what it means.

For some reason, I leave work early in the afternoon without telling anyone because I intend to be back quickly, but I keep getting delayed.

I run into two young women walking. They don't see the impending tornado zooming toward them. I don't tell them nor do I call their attention to the other people nearby who are scurrying to get away. I am somewhat relieved, as I pass them, to note that even though they are somewhat nerdy and plain looking, they have enough sense to put a jacket on. The one is sharing the navy blue jacket with the other—kind of draping it over her shoulders too.

To my relief, the tornado does not hit where I am, but goes to the outer banks and does lots of damage. I remember thinking that my life could have been so very different if the tornado had not turned because a big tsunami could have formed and I was very close to the shore.

How nice it would be to soak up the water and let myself enjoy the beach, but I know I have to get back to work.

I continue my walk and find myself in an empty theater foyer where the person who wrote and produced the movie is there for its first showing. No one but me is there to watch it. And I was just there by accident. I think I tell him that and he wants me to stay but I can't because I have to get back to work. But then other people start arriving to see the film and I am vastly relieved and slip out without being noticed.

I continue on my way back to work and am increasingly agitated that I keep getting waylaid and diverted. I try running, but it still does not feel like my body is going fast enough or that I am making much progress, though my limbs are moving in a running motion.

I get on an elevator and there are two men and one woman. The woman pushes the button to get us moving, but instead the floor folds up around our feet and we grab onto these dangling pieces of cloth to prevent us from tumbling down the elevator shaft. I know not to look down the shaft because then I will be really frightened.

I don't think it will help, but lo and behold, I start screaming as loud as I can. Miraculously, the woman and I end up outside of the elevator in a hall where there are other people. I watch the floor of the elevator go from its curled position and turn into a cradle. It is yellow in color with a brown edge.

The woman leaves to go to a bris (circumcision) and I leave to go back to work.

Since I have been gone so long, I decide to just take the time I was gone and subtract it from my overtime built up, so I don't feel guilty about being gone so much longer than I thought I would be. And because it was under four hours, it would not qualify for sick time.

Delving into the Dream

For the fun of it, and to dabble in amateur psychoanalysis, I go searching online for dream interpretations.

This is what I find:

- Dreaming you are in an accident signifies unexpected change and upset. Life being threatened. Pent-up guilt that you are subconsciously punishing yourself over it. You may be harboring deep anxieties and fears. This dream may tell you to slow down before you hit disaster—to re-think or re-plan your course of action and set yourself on a better path.
- Something is no longer functional, but dead. Perhaps you need to let go of a relationship.
- The color yellow is a sign of confidence in yourself and your abilities even though you will encounter opposition.
- Brown is an auspicious color to dream about, signifying freedom, success, money, and happy and long-lasting union.
- An elevator denotes increased understanding. Descending elevators denote your misfortunes are crushing and discouraging you.
- Film means observation of your own life.
- Floor denotes foundation and the need to create some stability.
- Hallway signifies trying to find some connection.
- Tornado is a symbol of confusion, chaos and emotional upset, and could represent an uncontrollable change that will be occurring in your life.

Exhausted, I fall into a dreamless sleep.

And wake up refreshed, the following morning.

A Good Thing?

Outpatients at Fairwinds are weighed on a regular basis but we can't see what the scale says.

The staff tells us to eat when hungry and I am hungry at night.

It's no wonder—that was the time when I habitually binged and purged.

I compulsively restrict my calories throughout the day, saving them up for when the sun goes down.

I don't know whether that is a good idea, but I haven't mindlessly stuffed myself nor thrown it all back up so maybe it's a good thing.

HALT

I am anxious. I soon will be without outpatient support for two weeks. Being ED's love slave for forty-six years makes me feel like a battered woman. And though it has been a full moon cycle since I have binged and purged—and even though ED seems quiet and benign—I am not completely reassured. His power force can erupt at any time, often without warning. His command over me conjures up images of an uncontrollable epileptic seizure erupting from my body.

I am no fool. I know what works for me: accountability. Knowing that three days a week I am an outpatient at Fairwinds.

The Gestalt theory is in place here, the whole being greater than the sum of its parts. Ironically, it's one of the very few things I remember verbatim from college psych. It's not any one component—group therapy, individual therapy, art therapy, nutritional class, weigh-in time, group dining—that keeps me on course. It's the eating disorder treatment program in its entirety—being present and watchful—that keeps me in a constructive, energized and proactive mode. Binge- and purge-free.

I have two weeks looming ahead without intensive outpatient treatment and support. Can I make it on my own?

I am traveling to the New York area to see three of my sons, two daughters-in-law and all my grandchildren. When I think of spending jam-packed time with my adult children and their families, I imagine an oil painting of a nature scene, sprouting colors of bright orange and intense purple. It is a scene ripe with intensity and promise, reflecting the yearning in me for a sustained and highly pleasurable connection with those I love so passionately. Will I be able to maintain my serenity if my high expectations aren't met?

"What is your biggest concern?" Dr. B asks. "Your biggest fear? The negative behavior you most want to avoid if things don't go perfectly?"

"Overeating to compensate for unfilled yearnings for more intimacy and closeness," I shoot back automatically.

"Well, what are the consequences for you of overeating?" She continues to probe.

I pause to consider. "Well, of course, the likelihood of purging increases. But also bloat, weight gain, disgust," I carefully list. "Oh yes, and disappointment, bad mood, discomfort and indigestion. And asking myself the same old question I always ask after a failed intervention: Why do I put myself through all this?"

"Hopefully, through treatment, you will move closer to an answer," Dr. B murmurs kindly. "For now, though, what can you do to prevent bingeing?" she prods.

I ponder this before replying.

"I guess I can practice mindful eating, as opposed to unconscious eating. You know, what we are learning here—to be aware of what we put into our mouths. Slowing down and savoring the experience of tasting, chewing, swallowing."

Dr. B remains silent.

I hesitate.

"Hmmm, what else did I learn?" I ask myself out loud. "Oh yes," I exclaim excitedly. "Keep safe snacks ready on standby for when I start to feel ravenous," I blurt out triumphantly.

Dr. B knits her brows, her mouth in a firm grimace.

"Did I say something wrong?" I ask Dr. B, my body flooding with trepidation.

"No, Iris," she replies softly and patiently. "But you omitted an acronym that we here at Fairwinds pay great homage to: HALT."

- Hunger
- Anger
- Loneliness
- Tiredness

She is right. As I am poised on the brink of a two-week journey, I need to hold that concept close. I need to internalize that the only thing HALT does in relation to binges is start one, not halt one.

Rummaging Through the Humor Drawer

I am hurriedly searching through the masses of funny quips I continuously rip out of magazines and print off of websites, and then unceremoniously dump in my oversized kitchen cutlery drawer. I am in need of some lighthearted diversion, as soon I will be boarding a plane to the land of the yearning—New York City.

Why do I call it the land of the yearning? Because all five of my grandchildren and three of my sons live there. I stay with each of them for about two days. I arrive knowing that already I want more than I will get. And I leave each one of them yearning for more.

Instead of coping with my uncomfortable feelings by bingeing, I steel myself to lower my expectations, climb out of my self-absorbed silo and get over the tendency to over-personalize slights. I am looking toward humor as a tool to help me soothe my soul. To help me set realistic expectations. To help me simply relax and enjoy my family.

Ironically, the first thing I grab from the humor drawer is a piece about kids and their moms, once more displaying the differences between sons and daughters.

I begin to read:

This is what little *GIRLS* say about their mothers:

> Be a mother. It's a rewarding thing. Mothers and Chanukah are the two best things in the world. And my mother is the best gift I ever got.—Rachel (age nine)

> Dear Mother,
> You are the best mother a kid could have. I think you are beautiful and very kind too. I hope I turn out to be as good a mother as you. I want to make you a proud grandma with no gray hairs or worries. Love,—Jenny (age nine)

> My mom makes great matzoh ball soup. Our family always eats it at Christmas time.—Carey (age seven)

This is what little *BOYS* say about their mothers:

> Can you believe that my mother doesn't know where a linebacker lines up in football? She needs to learn more about the real world.—Michael (age nine)

> Dear Mummy,
> Want to make a deal? You clean up my room for me and I'll start listening to you. What do you say? Greetings,—Adam (age seven)

> Mother,
> I won't tell Dad you lost a hundred dollars on lottery tickets. But that was a dumb way to spend Mother's Day.—Jason (age seven)

Dear Mom,

So what if you're fat like a dinosaur? You're still the greatest.

Happy Mother's Day. Your little aggravation—Abe (age nine)

By the time the cab drops me off at the airport, my step is bouncy, my smile contagious and my confidence level high. I just have this innate feeling that my trip will be lighter on yearning and heavier on sheer enjoyment. That's the power of humor to lift flagging spirits. And I am not disappointed.

No Option

It's Wednesday, March 14, 2012. I am determined to wring everything out of this program I can so that I don't ever have to go back.

Looking Out the Window

The days fly by. Therapy progresses. Disturbing realizations spring to the surface of my mind.

I begin to observe things I haven't paid much attention to before. Women my age—and generally any over fifty—seem to be inordinately bothered by their weight. No matter if they wear size four yoga pants or a size sixteen housedress, body distress is evident.

As my friend Pam, who's been selling women's apparel for decades, tells me, "All women complain about their bodies."

Maybe, I surmise, we have too much time on our hands. I scrutinize my peers' situations closely. They seem more isolated than ever before. No more parent associations to join. Soccer games to attend. Children to chauffeur.

I must have had an inkling of the empty nest sorrow waiting for me around the bend, as I wrote the following words in a column over twenty years ago.

I rinse peanut butter off the knife and put it in the dishwasher.

I scrub dried mozzarella cheese from a plate and put it in the dishwasher too.

I scrape carrot after carrot and painstakingly cut them into thin strips.

I slice bagels for sandwiches, snacks, mini-pizzas and quick pick-me-ups.

And all the time I look out the kitchen window.

I see my children playing Wiffle ball in the summer, their brows dripping with sweat.

I see my children tossing a football in the fall, their feet slipping on the golden leaves.

I see my children building snowmen in the winter, impatiently discarding scarves and hats as their cheeks get redder and their bodies warmer.

I see my children pounding tennis balls against the garage wall in the spring, using muscles that have lain dormant over the winter.

Sometimes it's painful to look out the kitchen window.

I fry dozens of hamburgers and fill dozens of ceramic pitchers full of fresh lemonade for Max's first party with girls.

I pop kernels and kernels and kernels of popcorn for after-school snacks and Sunday football game gatherings.

I bake birthday cupcakes for Louie's party, painstakingly decorating each one with his name.

I melt bags of colored chocolate to mold into Valentine hearts for each of my sons and their buddies.

And all the time, I look out my kitchen window.

I see Harry teaching Frank how to properly load books, computer, and clothes into the car he'll drive up to college.

I see Frank teaching Max how to back the car out of the garage without hitting the tree (and his other brothers).

I see Max teaching Sam how to start the lawn mower after the motor is flooded.

I see Sam teaching Lou how to rake, bag and dump the leaves in fall and the grass clippings in summer.

Sometimes it's painful to look out the kitchen window and realize that one day there will be no more lunches to pack, carrots to scrape, kernels to pop, hamburgers to fry, and children to watch.

I am a mother whose back seat of her car was now empty. What I didn't perceive back then was that physical emptiness would lead to an emotional emptiness—disconnecting me from friends and acquaintances and insidiously impacting my own routine and sense of stability. What I didn't perceive back then is that disconnection would also lead to isolation, even from my own self.

Now that I had free time, I focused on counting calories and critiquing my body parts more rigorously than ever. I spent hours trying on old and new outfits—searching for the creeping ravages of age. And that was only from the outside. I incessantly searched for signs of the irreversible damage on the inside—damage I may have done to my teeth, my heart, my throat and my stomach from vomiting daily. A tooth sensitive to cold would turn into a root canal, accompanied by a dry socket. A twinge in my heart was a sure sign of impending heart failure. A sore throat became linked to esophageal cancer. A stomachache was the first sign of a ruptured stomach.

I chose wallowing in self-imposed misery about my flabby stomach, jiggly kneecaps, and sagging chin line. I chose ridding myself of negative emotions by flushing them down the toilet.

Therapy forced me to screech to a halt. Therapy forced me to come to terms with the stark fact that my childhood was long past over, as was my reproductive life and child rearing years. Therapy forced me to confront my demons of low self-esteem and lack of meaningful and safe connections. Therapy forced me to face the embarrassment and shame centered on my inability to just "grow out of my eating disorder."

Therapy forced me to forge new paths to recovery. To modify my behaviors. To implement healthy habits. And, of course, to write.

Nine P.M.

Nine p.m. is cut-off time.
    Time to stop tidying up.
    Time to stop misting the plants.
    Time to stop organizing yet another closet.
    Time to stop proofreading a future column.
    Time to stop fitting in one more arm exercise routine.
    Nine p.m. is the start of down time. Rewarding myself with a
        few indulgences.
    Like delving into a newly bought novel.
    Like binge watching a few of my favorite TV series.
    Like knitting yet another shawl.
    Like sipping some wine or popping some popcorn.
    Lighting a candle and dimming the lights.
    And when I spot ED's shadowy presence peering through my family room window, I pull down the shades and beat a hasty retreat to my second floor loft.

Converse Sneakers

One day folds into the next. I honor my commitment to the outpatient eating disorder program by showing up and wholeheartedly participating. I honor and sustain my no-binge/no-purge pledge to myself by altering some of my nightly patterns.

I no longer sprawl out on the family room couch each evening—the same couch that is just a few feet from the kitchen and in clear view of the mason jars lining my granite counters—mason jars filled with treats my family adores: giant gumballs, individually wrapped chocolate kisses and extra-salty sunflower seeds. Instead, I climb the stairs to the loft—a more secluded and inaccessible space—and hang out there watching TV.

And I don't indulge in my usual selections of national and international news programs anchored by familiar faces. I shun interview formats with stimulating talk show hosts and switch channels when any program smacking of self-improvement appears. I don't want to be educated or enlightened. I just want to be mindlessly enthralled with something I can lose myself in night after night.

God bless binge-watching—one of the newer offshoots of the technological advances we enjoy today. *Grey's Anatomy* is my "drug of choice." I am enthralled with Meredith's struggles, Izzy's idiosyncrasies and George's problems with self-esteem.

Grey's Anatomy provides me with continuous diversion during the very critical months of my outpatient treatment. I have instituted a preemptive plan. When *Grey's Anatomy* ends, I will binge on *The Good Wife* and *Parenthood*.

I used to eagerly await the nine p.m. clock chimes, because it signified pantry raid time. Now, at that same hour, I remove myself from the temptation to stuff my body with food. Avoiding the kitchen, I climb the stairs to the loft. I stay in my safety net all evening, immersed in other people's heartaches and triumphs, wrapped in a cocoon of my own making. Watching three to four segments of *Grey's Anatomy* each evening eats up the scary nighttime hours until bed.

Glimpsing glimmers of success, I decide to indulge in a little more therapy—retail, that is. Instead of sitting down with a pint of chocolate chip ice cream and a package of crunchy butter cookies as a reward, I decide to buy myself something wearable, something I would not ordinarily purchase. I ponder. I flip through magazines. Search Internet apparel sites. I spot the shoes immediately and gleefully know I have located just the right gift for myself: classic high top Converse sneakers. I immediately order two pairs—one in bight cherry red and the other in black.

Though I do not know it at the time, the five-pointed star insignia on the outside of each Converse shoe signifies connection to the elements. How ironic that in the days to follow I would soon be learning the importance of connection—and the devastating effects lack of connection spawns.

I wear the red ones to group therapy the very next day.

Small Victory

I am becoming enamored with the small victory. I am becoming leery of the unsustainable giant leaps of grandiose behavior changes.

And I am fiercely courting gratitude—gratitude for these toddling baby steps I am taking on the road to my recovery.

Finding other outlets for pleasure—not just those emanating from the dinner table—awakens long-dormant talents and interests. I rummage in the cavernous closet under my stairs and cart out knitting needles in all sizes, and yarn in all colors and weights. Knitting and purling becomes an activity that, along with binge-watching TV, helps me weave through the danger zone of the evening hours—the hours I always spent bingeing and purging.

Little did I know that knitting would soon not only continue to provide me with solace, but give solace to others, too.

Knitting Keeps Us from Unraveling

Cranston was released from inpatient treatment last week and spent the next seven days bingeing, purging and drinking alone in the one-bedroom, un-air-conditioned apartment she rents with her boyfriend, the sub-literary brute who works at a beach hamburger shack down the road from our treatment center.

"Thank goodness," I tell myself, "I only have one substance abuse issue—food "

Others in here, I am finding, have alcohol and drug issues—some, even cutting issues. Mine is just food, glorious food. In a sense, I am fortunate: I don't have to stop eating, like others have to stop their vices all together. My path to freedom lies in re-orienting and re-training myself to view food as a source of sustenance, fuel, and yes, even pleasure.

Following her relapse, Cranston shows up in outpatient therapy. I eye her warily. She is a mess. Despondent. Disgusted. Despairing and disappointed. Her mouth is slack, her eyes glazed, her hair tangled, her complexion pasty.

My first reaction is to turn away. Self-protect—as if her stumbling is contagious. I recoil in fear, moving closer to my chum Ari, who is inappropriately infatuated with an older fellow, an adjunct math professor at the local community college.

"What do you like to do, Cranston," our group leader probes gently, "in your free time?"

Her question is met with silence. I detect a stiffening of Cranston's shoulders.

I am almost at the point of not listening to her interaction with the group leader, when something Cranston murmurs catches my attention.

"I like to do things with my hands," Cranston replies, rather sheepishly. "When I was a little girl," she continues meekly, "I liked those looms you bought at the dime store—the ones that made those colorful pot holders you gave your mom on Mother's Day."

"Try knitting," I call out, with a touch of sarcasm. "It's hard to binge and drink when you are holding two knitting needles in your hands."

My companions laugh. And to my surprise, Cranston's deer-caught-in-a-headlight gaze fades just a tad.

The next night I bring her an old striped beach bag filled with knitting needles, three balls of different colors of yarn and an instruction book. I hand it to her, uncertain of her reaction.

A broad smile appears on her pinched face, as she tentatively reaches out for my gift. And I realize how very pretty she really is.

Crossing the Ravine

I am raging and frustrated.

The orthopedist prescribed steroids for the pain in my legs due to arthritis. When I picked up the pills from the druggist, I avidly scanned the enclosed sheet, looking for the side effects. Weight gain was one of them. I still took the pills.

The orthopedist also suggested that I stop walking up and down my staircase as a preferred form of daily exercise. I complied.

Two weeks later, I pull my brown skirt with the white polka dots from the closet. I slip it on. Actually, I try to slip it on. Instead, I struggle to get it over my hips and buttoned at the waist. The fit's uncomfortable, signaling what I have already surmised: a few more pounds packed on.

I am crazy and irritable.

And it doesn't help that my supervisor at work is constantly on my back, that my friends are pestering me to have dinner and can't understand why I continue to decline. It doesn't help that my house seems dirtier and messier since my evenings are spent in therapy, and spats with my husband now lead to stand-offs. And that my bank account reserves are dwindling as fast as my optimistic spirit.

All the pressures I normally could contain with a modicum of healthy perspective and a bit of good humor have mounted exorbitantly—causing me to pause and wonder where all this bubbling angst is springing from.

Ha ha. That's not complicated: the increasingly snug fit of my brown skirt with the white polka dots.

I am struggling between past bad habits and future healthy ones. Being heavy is not an option, nor is bingeing and purging. I am not supposed to diet because deprivation leads to overeating. I am not supposed to binge and purge because that could ultimately lead to death. So, how do I reverse the scale's direction?

A Heavier Me

I muster the fortitude to weigh myself, in spite of admonishments to the contrary from the treatment center staff. Normally the scale hovers at 130, but this time the needle settles at 144 pounds.

I stare at the marker in horror and disbelief, willing it to shift downward. It stays at 144.

A restless night ensues.

Along with this unwelcome development, I recognize I also need to negotiate a truce between the vision of me at my ideal weight and the vision of me as I am. I need to develop healthier signs of a life well lived—not measured by the girth of my hips and the looseness of my inner thigh skin.

I ponder the quandary: Do I have to accept that a heavier me is the new normal? I just can't.

The next evening, I gingerly approach the dietician at the treatment center. "I'm kind of frustrated," I mutter. "You guys don't want us getting weighed while in treatment. I get the feeling I need to say 'No' to diets, but to practice a kind of free-range eating that should at some point stabilize weight and diminish cravings.

"Well," I continue shrilly, hot tears beginning to course down my cheeks, "I've gained almost fourteen pounds and that cannot continue. It cannot continue."

"What seems to be the problem?" she inquires gently.

"Well, I'm getting better at recognizing stomach rumbles and eating soon after," I reply, "but portion control is still a struggle."

"Buy yourself a gym membership," she laughingly declares. "Honestly, join a gym, eat what you are eating and see how adding an exercise component impacts things."

I really hate gyms, but I love to walk. So here's my modest plan: walking every morning, religiously beginning with thirty minutes per day and building up to sixty.

It has been about seven weeks since ED reared his ugly head and if I can tame that lurking monster, I ought to be able to achieve this goal too.

Tangling With a Bunch of Stuff on April 15th

Outpatient therapy continues and my energy level surges upward.

Sleep is elusive. My husband, knowing how radically and thoroughly I have dedicated myself to a victorious outcome from outpatient therapy for my bulimia, worries that I am becoming manic. I brush off his concerns as I clean closets with vigor and file the mound of papers stacked up for years in nooks and crannies all over the house. I sweep the garage at midnight. I polish all my grandmother's silver to a high sheen.

Admittedly, I too worry just a tad about my high spirits and rushes of adrenaline. I just keep going, hoping it's in "normal" limits.

And praying my manic activity will keep the memory of a day, thirty-seven years ago, at bay.

Dear Andrea,

Well, it's an April 15th again. It's been thirty-seven years since I've seen you. That last fateful morning, you went out to lunch and shopping; I went into surgery. Ironically, I survived the surgery—you didn't survive the lunch.

No one knows exactly what happened. Was your radio too loud? Were your reflexes too slow? It was obvious from the TV news coverage, which showed your smashed-up car, that you never had a chance against the train.

Thirty-seven years...your husband's remarried, divorced, remarried and separated...your babies are grown...your best friend's moved away. And moved back again.

Time has dimmed the memory of you and eased the pain, but I never sail nonchalantly over railroad crossings nor hear your name without recalling your generous heart and your fun-loving spirit.

Thirty-seven years...your sons are long past Bar Mitzvah age. I watched your parents dance together in perfect rhythm at your youngest son's wedding many springs ago, and though your brother's wife told me your mom had Alzheimer's, I didn't totally believe her. When she saw my face after all those years, and I mentioned your name, her smile went all the way up to her eyes.

Time has dimmed the memory of you and eased the pain, but I never see good friends lunching and laughing without a twinge. And I never think of all the years of living you've missed, each year when I mark your birthday by buying myself a single, long-stemmed red rose.

Thirty-seven years...your grandfather's long dead; your brother's first-born daughter, whom he named after you, has already graduated from college. Your sons have both been happily married for over a decade—to women, I wistfully hope, who fill the void your death so prematurely left in them. And, you are now a grandmother—many times over.

To me, dear Andrea, you'll always be twenty-seven—vivacious, naive and irrepressible—with your big, beautiful blue eyes and your unruly head of chestnut colored hair. But, it may surprise you to know your best friend is now sixty-seven—and a little wiser, and a tad more subdued.

I've learned many things in the years since I've lost you, Andrea, but the two things that seem to always hover close are:

Don't tangle with trains.

Best friends are forever.

The Pull of the Chew

Chewing gum helps when I feel like I need to eat even though I know I am not physically hungry.

And I am chewing a lot of gum.

This Is What I Notice

At intervals of about every three to four hours, my appetite intensifies. When I am fighting fatigue, I reach for something sweet and then something salty.

When I am frustrated, my mouth cavity starts to salivate no matter what time it is, no matter how long it's been since I have last eaten.

When I am angry, annoyed or irritable, feeling hungry is my salient greeting.

When I am introspective, I ask myself why I will not allow myself to attain what I most covet: a slimmer body.

The weeks pass. I am not bingeing and purging.

This is what I notice: My clothes fit tighter. My hips are wider. My face is fuller.

This is what I am no longer acutely aware of: The length of time that has passed since ED came courting.

Shed the Armor

As I participate in group therapy, I notice a few disturbing things about my behavior. I like to crack jokes and divert the attention away from myself. I am more comfortable reaching out to nurture others than I am exposing my own shortcomings and imperfections.

I like to give the impression I am in control, that I am perfect or damn near it. I want others to believe I am coping and I am not in need.

Group therapy belies this mindset. Chips away at my shield. Tarnishes my armor. Until I must shed what so far in life has shielded my gaping vulnerability.

Group therapy demands an inner accounting. It is not a cushioned atmosphere.

Bank account balances don't matter, nor do stellar credit ratings.

Nor your proficiency level at tennis, or your grade point average, or your college transcript.

It's a pure, though contrived, island of bohemia where all that matters is the atrophied bags of bones occupying the plastic chairs.

I must learn to:

Ask for what I want

Ask for what I need

Articulate what I am feeling

I practice it over and over again until it begins to feel more comfortable and natural.

It takes a long time.

And Then...

In treatment, I realize I am a serial cheater. I cheated on my first husband. And I cheated on my second husband too. Both times with my lover, ED.

Let it be noted: Neither my first husband, Gary, or my present husband, Steven, is a weak man. But they were powerless against the strength and endurance of ED.

Long before the media introduced us to eating disorders, my first husband was dimly aware that I was a little quirky in my eating habits. When I ate too much, I would go in the bathroom and throw it up. But as the frequency of my odd actions grew, he became more concerned that something was seriously askew. One day for dinner, I ate a huge sirloin steak, baked potato, onion rings and two pieces of pecan pie. Then I guzzled down twenty-four ounces of ice cold Coke. Groggily, in a full-fledged food-induced coma, with my stomach uncomfortably bulging against my jeans, I flung myself out of the kitchen. I hastily retreated to the half bath to relieve myself of that stifling feeling of fullness and all those nasty calories I had just wolfed down. Uncharacteristically, my husband did not remain at the table, complacently finishing his meal, but followed me. I slammed the door in his face, quickly locking him out and turned toward the toilet.

"Iris," he yelled through the hollow-core door, "if you throw up what you just ate, I'm leaving the house."

"Goodbye. See ya. Get going," I shouted after him, at the top of my lungs—half of me in a state of hysteria because he was trying to stop me, and half of me in a state of relief that his effort had failed. Turning on the spigot full blast, I planted my two feet on either side of the commode and proceeded to throw my guts up. He left the house and didn't return until way past midnight. When he did, I was fast asleep, exhausted by my bingeing and purging, and his unexpected reaction.

In the morning, neither of us spoke about it. Nor did he ever again try to stop me. I purposefully made it a point to wait until he went to bed to binge and purge. Or when he was at work. Or when our two toddlers were taking their naps. Never in front of him and never directly after a meal.

Years later, long after our divorce (unrelated to my bulimia), he gingerly asked me if I was still "doing it." I laughed uneasily and said, "I'm doing better." We both knew I was lying.

Because ED outlasted my first marriage, I was determined that he would not have any power over my second one. Simply, because I was unable to stop the binge/purge cycle, I had to keep my second husband out of the loop of my bizarre behavior. I couldn't risk making ED a contender in our marriage because I knew ED could win. And there was no way I could live without either of "my men." So in all the many years of my marriage to Steven—a marriage that continues to this day—it was a subject I wouldn't discuss—a battle I wouldn't let him help me wage. I wanted to keep this wonderful man as my husband. Not my warden. Not my fellow warrior against my great adversary. Because I was always afraid I would lose the battle and I couldn't risk losing Steven too.

Maybe

"Maybe she'd always wished to be beautiful and didn't quite dare to, because she could tell that people didn't say she was and more attention was given to other women, but she still had a frail hope that there'd been a mistake and she was after all. That was why from years of living on intelligence alone, when Eli told her she already had what she hadn't been able even to admit she dreamed of—that must have acted like a drug, flooding her with irresistible relief...maybe every single female, smart or not, couldn't help wanting that."—From *Casebook* by Mona Simpson.

We all seemed to crave beauty. We all seemed to equate thinness with beauty.

It was always what I wanted. Strived for. Fell short of achieving. And when I was close—almost there—got the utmost of positive feedback, attention and praise.

Who could resist that pull? I couldn't.

Who Ya Gonna Call?

I put the assignment off as long as I could. I watched CBS News' *Sunday Morning* hosted by Charles Osgood. Flipped through the pages of the *New York Times* with thoroughness I hadn't exhibited in years. Read every column in the Sunday Styles section. Drank my coffee. Ate my oatmeal. Called my mom. Restlessly paced my cavernous front hall. Sighed. And finally, faced the arduous homework assignment from Fairwinds. If needed, who would I call for help? And list ten enjoyable things I like to do.

I borrowed and then employed a technique called "sandboxing," which I loosely defined in my situation as a process of separating this exercise out from other recovery exercises. Since this particular assignment was wading into untried and uncharted territory for me, I needed some space to develop my lists.

Who would I call for help?

I sauntered into my book-lined living room with its soothing sage green color scheme and began contemplating the question at hand. What was immediately interesting about this first exercise was that it was so easy to come up with the people I would not choose to place on my call-for-help list:

All five of my adult kids. Inappropriate to burden them.

My husband. I didn't want him to morph into my policeman; I wanted him to remain my lover.

My mother. I didn't want to have to comfort her over my addiction, when I needed so badly the comfort and support myself.

Not one person from my family made the list as there was way too much baggage and emotion tied up in that arena. Not even my baby sister, my usual go-to confidant extraordinaire, was considered. Calling my immediate family would cause them great anguish. Sparing them was a form of self-protection too, as I wanted to avoid the genetic trigger conversations. In addition, confiding in them my "secret" would place them in the precarious ethical position of perhaps having to lie to other family members.

Who would I call for help?

Not surprisingly, I chose only people who had battled addictions and were victorious. People who had already adamantly urged me to call them whenever I needed a lifeline of support.

Tawny, my friend since grade school, who began her bingeing and purging during her freshman year of college and successfully overcame it years ago.

Joy, my seventy-year-old new friend who has been bulimia-free for one year and credits her practice of yoga for her success.

Gopal, a master gardener, a practicing physician, a gay man, and my newest friend, who just happens to live right across the street from me.

I could only think of three.

Ten enjoyable things I liked to do.

Sheepishly, I admit this exercise was less rigorous, but equally challenging. Plunking down on the grass in my front yard, I reluctantly faced the reality that bingeing and purging had been my primary source of pleasure (and pain) for so many years that it was tough to zero in on pleasurable pursuits not entirely related to, and centered around, food. But I gave it a whirl:

1. Taking a hot, bubbly bath while listening to singer Norah Jones

2. Gazing down at the bustling street scene from my second-story porch

3. Sipping a glass of wine while rocking in my antique, off-white rocker

4. Retail therapy (Duh—Who doesn't respond positively to that?)

5. Immersing myself in a novel, heavy on both plot and character development

6. Spending a Saturday afternoon with my husband exploring somewhere new

7. Planning house improvements

8. Having a substantive conversation with each of my sons

9. A few unbroken hours with each of my grandchildren

10. Sharing holidays with my family

11. Lunch with a friend

12. Writing a really good column

13. Knitting prayer shawls for those in distress

14. Learning something new

Wow. The list was longer than I expected and larger than needed. I was eager to embrace the next step in my recovery.

It's Never Too Late

As reported in the *Tampa Bay Times*:

After thirty-five years of futile efforts to become the first person to swim from Cuba to Key West without the aid of a protective shark cage, she successfully navigated 110 miles across the Florida straits.

She was a year away from becoming Medicare eligible and two years removed from being able to collect her full social security benefits.

Four previous efforts had failed. Calm weather conditions and the addition of a specially constructed face mask to protect her from jellyfish stings allowed her to make the crossing after fifty-two hours and fifty-four minutes in the water.

Upon completion, she delivered three messages in Key West:
Never give up.
You are never too old to chase a dream.
Teamwork is important.
Diana Nyad—my age, my hero.

Real Estate in Your Head

Amy Poehler states in her book *Yes Please*, "I need to conserve the amount of real estate I let people take up in my heart and brain."
ED took up the real estate in my head.

I was the Grantor, giving away ownership of my property.

ED was the Grantee, given ownership of the gross area of my property. He occupied the sum total of all my bodily space.

As soon as his tenancy began, I experienced Functional Obsolescence, a decrease in my value due to a feature which renders me undesirable: ED's presence. His residence changed my landscape, rendering it unusable for its originally intended purpose—to feed and sustain me.

Legal Description: White, Jewish female, age sixty-four, approximately five feet, two inches, 144 pounds.

On-Site Improvements contribute to the said property's value and are as follows: shellacked nails, contact lenses, enhanced hair color, capped teeth and shaved appendages.

Subject property's facade is artificial and inconsistent with the construction of the subject's interior.

Please note existence of present tenant sharing occupancy in said property is a non-conforming use, contrary to zoning specifications and owner's desire.

Past attempts to transfer ownership of tenancy to more appropriate renters has failed. Lease negotiations ended in a stalemate. Offers of relocation services have been turned down by the current tenant, as have any attempts at remodeling said structure to improve the value or desirability of said property.

At present, the long-term agreement between Grantor and Grantee remains in force, even though Grantor has at times expressed the desire to break it.

Grantee maintains he has the right to occupy the property and that it is a single family property designed and built to support the habitation of one family—his.

Title search was completed and research of property's title history ensures that the property is unencumbered, with no additional claims or liens, except from present tenant, who has resided in subject property for forty-six years and expressing no wish to relocate.

A walk-through of said property shows minor wear and tear, consistent with everyday use.

Grantor concedes said property at this time is under-improved and expresses interest in developing it into something more compatible with the existing neighborhood. Grantor also concedes that the property has not been improved to the full extent of its potential and expresses a strong desire to do so.

Present tenant requests no transfer of ownership at this time and threatens legal action if Grantor proceeds with development plans.

Appraiser's estimate of value: Property is poised for great increase in value if the existing tenant can be evicted from the property before substantial physical deterioration occurs.

Eviction process begins in 2011. Grantee's defense folds.

Grantee's tenancy is terminated on February 14, 2012. He leaves no forwarding address.

A Cobbled Together History of Bulimia

When I became embroiled in the binge/purge cycle, there was simply no word to describe my action.

From Dipsy's World:

People from different nations around the world throughout the years have practiced strange eating habits. For example, the Egyptians believed and engaged in monthly purges in attempts to remain healthy. The Romans created a place called a vomitorium where men would empty their stomachs so they could continue to eat, basically stuffing themselves at each sitting.

During ancient Greek and Roman times, Bulimlia, which was the term for "ox-like hunger" was widely practiced among people. As early as the 18th century, "La Boulimie" was used in French literature to describe this pattern of overeating.

Prior to the 1970s, little was known about bulimia, even among psychiatrists. In the mid-1970s, bulimia was categorized and seen as a distinct illness. In 1970, an English psychiatrist from London, Dr. Gerald F. M. Russell, was the first to name the disorder bulimia nervosa. He described bulimia in a patient by noting the "patient suffers from powerful and intractable urges to overeat; the patient seeks to avoid the 'fattening' effects of food by inducing vomiting or abusing purgatives or both; the patient has a morbid fear of becoming obese."

In addition, he described the key clinical feature of bulimia in thirty patients he had seen between 1972 and 1978 as an "ominous variant of anorexia nervosa." His original description follows:

Episodes of overeating constituted the most constant feature of the disorder...overeating was often overshadowed by major dramatic clinical phenomena—intractable self-induced vomiting or purgation...the constancy and significance of overeating invite a new terminology for the description of this symptom—bulimia nervosa.

From Yahoo!

Ancient Roman people used to vomit up the food they ate in the period of feasting. Some other cultures, like the ancient Egyptians, purged themselves every month for three days in succession to preserve health. They thought that human disease came from food.

It doesn't seem like these ancient practices of bingeing and purging were the same as what we term bulimia now. There was no evidence of the drive for thinness that is the obvious trait in modern bulimics. In fact, skinny women were not the normal shape in that day and age.

From the evidence that has been reported, it is obvious that bulimia nervosa as it is presented now was an unknown disease until the late twentieth century. The motives in the past for overeating and then purging were different from today and the psychological aspects were also different.

Today, bulimia is seen as a coping mechanism for stress, for the intense pressure to look slim, for addictive tendencies, and for problems with impulse control.

Living in the Moment

The therapy session begins with the group leader boldly announcing the agenda for the evening: Living in the Moment.

I groan.

That concept is something I have been working on for a long time—especially living in the moment that is not stellar. Not ideal. Not perfect.

I think back to a past Thanksgiving weekend when I was wracked with misery. My favorite aunt had passed away—no longer with us to celebrate this holiday weekend. My oldest son was 1,000 miles away and wouldn't be here with his brothers—a first.

My middle son, his wife and new baby were moving away and wouldn't be as accessible as they were now. And I had a helluva week coming up—mostly filled with things I wasn't particularly keen on doing.

I tried to force myself to shed the past and shed the future, and look at the day in a vacuum: my parents were here and healthy, my husband and four other sons were upstairs sleeping, and my sister and her family were in from Virginia. Our Thanksgiving table would be full. If I looked at the day without the context of the past and without the lens to the future, there was no reason in the world not to feel wonderful!

That's when I began to understand what living in the moment entails:

- A mindset of "Wherever you go, there you are."
- A practice of wakefulness and mindfulness; not cruising on autopilot.
- A state of being on the playing field, rather than hanging out on the sidelines.
- A celebration of what is, not what was and not what you wish it to be.

It was not as easy as I had once thought—to live in the moment.

I hunt up a column I wrote on the subject for some additional encouragement.

I realize I devote no time to reading novels. Magazines take their place. No time to leisurely cook a meal from scratch. Carry-out makes a ubiquitous presence. No time to take a purposeless walk with a friend—I just pedal furiously on the newest exercise machine at the gym, while listening on headphones to CNN and checking text messages on my phone.

I live my life always anticipating the next deadline, rushing to meet overlapping obligations. Performing every task as fast and efficiently as possible with little regard for experiencing pleasure or satisfaction while doing so. Depriving myself of things in the past that have brought pleasure, grounding, and an exquisite sense of being in touch with what makes me feel good.

Another duty: New Year's resolutions—usually relegated to the "if I have time pile"—are this year subjected to a scrutinous inventory. My mind is yearning to sink into a plot- and character-driven novel. My fingers are itching to knit yet another shawl—to feel that rhythmic motion and watch as I create something of substance out of a benign-looking ball of yarn. But how can I justify the time?

Or, on the other hand, how can I not?

I draw inspiration from the late Erma Bombeck, who said if she had her life to live over, "I would have eaten the popcorn in the living room…and would have sat on the lawn with my children and not worried about grass stains…and burned the pink candle sculpted like a rose before it melted in storage."

I think of the guest towels and the fancy soaps in my first floor bath. And how irritated I get when my youngest son Louie and his friends use them. And how we have lived in our house for eleven years and never once used the living room fireplace.

This evening I vow to loosen up a little—to sort of gently rotate my shoulder blades and breathe deeply while taking the time to actually hear what my husband says to me as we both attempt to connect after a long day. I will stop myself from checking phone messages, emails, snail mail and hurriedly starting dinner. I will command myself to stand still, look straight at the man I married, and listen.

I am going to try hard to live in the moment.

I am going to isolate each event and celebrate it fully— without looking back or projecting ahead.

I am going to allow time for sighs of contentment and yelps of triumph.

The next time I see newspapers scattered all over and spot an apple core on the table beside the couch, or I see dust on the blinds *and couch pillows astray, I vow to close my eyes and re-work the scene. I will focus on my husband and children, sit down near where they are sitting, take part in what they are doing and relegate what needs to be done for a later time.*

My New Year's resolution is to abandon the title of Sultan of Busyness. For good.

That column was written on the eve of 2001. Maybe this year, I'll finally succeed.

Going Out to Dinner Was Always a Challenge

In the early years, my routine was simple. In college—which is when I started bingeing and purging—I would often go to Lum's (a hot dog diner) with my then boyfriend, Gary. I scanned the menu, ordered whatever I wanted, and gobbled it up. An hour later, curfew approaching, Gary dropped me off at my sorority house. He drove away and I headed for the sorority house's guest bathroom, adjacent to the front door, and vomited up my dinner. I then climbed the stairs to my bedroom and finished my math assignment. I guess the sounds of vomiting were loud enough at times to attract the attention of some of my more observant sorority sisters, but none ever commented on my strange behavior. After all, it was 1967. Who knew about eating disorders?

After Gary and I married and he began working full-time, our tastes in food elevated from hot dogs to steak and upscale Italian. No matter. My behavior remained constant. Scan the menu. Order whatever I wanted. Gobble it up. The difference in my behavior was in the way I purged. I had to be more strategic since we were now living together. After dessert, while Gary waited for the check, I'd slip away to the restroom. If the stalls were empty, I'd purge away. If they weren't, I'd wait until we got home. While he rifled through the day's mail and watched the eleven o'clock news, I would slink away and purge quickly.

Other occasions, of course, proved more problematic: friends' rehearsal dinners and weddings, extended family events, mini vacations. First, I'd scope out the purging possibilities and then, depending on what I discovered, plan my binges. Looking back, did I enjoy the celebrations and festivities? Certainly not as fully as I could have if ED had not been always lurking around.

As mentioned before, on the one occasion that Gary did actually confront me about my bizarre behavior, I shut him out. I adamantly refused—and continued to refuse—to discuss my slavish addiction. Not even when we went into intensive couples therapy in an effort to save our marriage did I relent and open up about my full-blown bulimic state.

Separation from my first husband, Gary, and our subsequent divorce left me free of an unhappy, unsatisfying union, but it also left me with a tremendous amount of unstructured time. I would like to say I used that time wisely—to confront my own shortcomings. To explore why I couldn't allow anyone to get truly close to me. To explore why I couldn't seem to tolerate criticism, imperfection or a chink or two in my carefully constructed armor. Instead, I used the time to numb myself from the painful emotions that emerged from the demise of my marriage. And what better way to numb myself than with food?

At this point in my life, my two toddlers napped in the afternoons. I remember taking quick trips to the local convenience store before nap time. I varied the locations I visited out of embarrassment over my purchases: Mars bars, caramel ripple ice cream and Oreo cookies. On one occasion, the counter clerk in my immediate neighborhood remembered me being in the week before, stocking up on high calorie, sugar-laden goodies. I panicked. "Oh," I quickly made up. "I have a card game at my house weekly and my friends love sweets."

When my divorce was final the following summer, I moved back to Cincinnati, where my parents and siblings were. I went to work full-time in my dad's real estate office. Purging during the day simply was not an option. That's when nightly bingeing and purging morphed into an ingrained habit. After a full day of work, sandwiched between morning and evening mothering duties with my two young sons, I was exhausted. I was stressed. I was lonely. After the kids' story time, I'd head for the kitchen, whip up a batch of cake batter from scratch and sit cross-legged on the living room couch. Mindlessly, with glazed eyes and limp body, I focused on two things: shoveling in the smooth, rich, creamy cake batter with an oversized wooden spoon, while listening for my kids—concerned that they would wander in and catch their mom in such a weird state.

Shortly thereafter, I started dating Steven, who I would wed the following summer. From the very beginning of our relationship, I knew this man was someone very special.

I'd like to say that falling utterly in love was a panacea and allowed me to wean myself from my hateful, insidious attraction to ED, but it wasn't. I lived in terror that I would in some way screw up this relationship with Steven. I lived in terror that he wouldn't love me if he knew the "real" me. So my bingeing and purging allowed me to keep my anxiety manageable. It was a strategy I would employ for years—corroding my ability to dialogue honestly with my husband. Rendering me unable to communicate my anger, my hurts, my disappointments—and sometimes even rage—that can bubble up and erupt in any relationship when feelings aren't aired.

Steven was a court administrator when we met. Soon after our marriage, he seized the opportunity to learn the real estate brokerage and appraisal business from my father. Steven was also a dedicated body builder who rigorously worked out five times per week. And he was a man adapting to the slippery slope of full-time step-parenting. It was no wonder that each evening, shortly after the boys' baths and story time, he too went to bed.

I loved those times.

The apartment was quiet. The toys were neatly stacked on their shelves. The dinner dishes were lined up neatly in the dishwasher. And the three most important "men" in my life were safely ensconced nearby. Looking back, I am filled with both sadness and regret—that I couldn't savor the evening hours, aglow in my good fortune. Instead I chose ED. I began with quickly foraging in the pantry for all the goodies I had stashed out of sight when putting away the groceries. I lined up my array of foods. I binged. I purged. I showered. I took off my makeup. I brushed, flossed and gargled. I fell into an exhausted heap beside my new husband.

This routine went on for years. It went on after we moved from our first apartment into a brand new house in the suburbs. It went on during each of my three subsequent pregnancies as three more sons were added to our family. It went on when I quit working full-time and devoted myself to publishing a parenting newspaper, writing a slice-of-life column and co-parenting all five boys.

So painful was my secret that even now I cannot accurately recall when I confessed to Steven my dirty little habit. Nor why I did.

How's that for denial?

Swiveling the Rubik's Cube

I grow suspicious of my friends. The more I learn of the hidden life of bulimics, the more I scrutinize my friends' relationships with food. Could others I am close to also have an eating disorder? I seem to have concealed my bingeing and purging for years. Why do I assume I'm the only one harboring this monster?

Could it be my skinny friend who, after placing a tiny morsel of carrot cake into her mouth, announces that she hasn't had a piece of cake in twenty-one years and then swallows it quickly?

Could it be the friend I ate lunch with regularly over an eighteen-year period and never once saw her order anything but a salad—without dressing yet—even though she vigorously professed to hate salads?

Or the one who opens the tiniest bag of chocolate-covered raisins she can find and puts one in her mouth, throwing the next one out the car window—continuing this rhythm until the bag is empty?

Or could it be the one who disappears to the ladies' room after every meal and returns smelling of breath mints?

Or the one who lost sixty pounds in her thirties and managed to keep it off for decades, even when I watch her eat two and three desserts at a sitting?

I wonder. I watch.

I re-work and revise.

But I don't approach.

What Being Thin Means

Girdles. Push-up bras. Padded bras. Spandex. Control-top pantyhose. Tummy-tuckers.

I long to take a vacation from the constraints of clothing designed to minimize flaws and accentuate assets. I would like to just give notice to my flirty ta-tas and celebrate the bounciness of my jiggly behind without all the equipment.

I would like to be less slavishly addicted to the newest fat removal remedies.

Of course, such wild abandon screams self-confidence, bespeaks wholesomeness and reflects an uncontrived aura. Alas it can't be pulled off in a flattering way if I am fat. I know this.

But if I keep my body at a weight I am comfortable with, without employing all the construction site gizmos designed to lift, squeeze, smooth and compact, I invite people to look at me more as a person and less as a body of wonder.

And, in order to achieve this freeing feat, we all have to be comfortable with our bodies.

I did an informal survey with my close friends, most—if not all—of whom are impacted negatively when they gain weight, and very happy when they lose it.

I asked them what being thin means to them.

Sherry: "I like to be on the thin side because it's all about making me feel and look younger."

Ida: "I get noticed."

Jessie: "It's freedom from worrying about the package and from fashion constraints."

Susan: "Being thin means to me that I can wear anything hanging in my closet and wear it well."

Jackie: "I can shop without a pit in my stomach."

Alicia: "When I know I look good (i.e. thin), I stop obsessing over how I look and let the rest go. I am more efficient, focused and productive. I look forward to going to social outings, not because I need to be the most stunning person in the room, but because I know I look the best that I can. I just flourish—it's empowering and freeing."

Laurin: "Being thin to me means not being invisible. Clerks at the grocery store, nail techs at the nail salons, the cashier at the corner market, the teller at the bank—they all remember me. It's not just because I am at a weight I am happy with—it's because when I am at a weight I am happy with, I feel good about myself, my life, my personality. And that comes through—people pick up on that."

Melanie: "Being thin results in my cheekbones being more prominent, so I wear less makeup. I don't contour my face with blush to achieve the illusion of cheekbones—I've got them. And lots of attention."

Ruth Harriet Jacobs, an author I once interviewed, said one of the perks of aging is that you can crash posh swimming pools in South Florida without hired help hounding you. Why? "Because," she relates, "no one pays any attention to the elderly lady wearing a faded bathing suit with a skirt." I wish she were still alive so I could ask her if she was okay with that, as long as she didn't look fat.

When I Lose Weight, My Life Will Change

Years ago, *Glamour* magazine did a three-page body image survey. The most striking finding from the survey was the universality of feeling too fat, no matter what a woman's actual weight was.

Married or single, employed or not—at all ages, education and income levels, a steady seventy-five percent of respondents felt they were too fat.

That was me.

Feelings about the difference ten fewer pounds would make in the quality of one's life leads to a pervasive feeling of dissatisfaction. "There isn't a day I don't wish I were thinner" is a typical comment.

Symptomatic with the near obsession with weight, when asked what would make a person happiest—losing weight, hearing from an old friend, a date with a man you admire or success at work—far more respondents chose losing weight (42%) then dating (21%), work success (22%) or hearing from an old friend (15%).

That was me.

Musings on My Mother

My mother was intent on raising a healthy kid—no small feat considering polio was a very real threat in the 1950s.

Who could blame her? Her philosophy made sense: A mother owed it to her child to give them the best start in life and feeding them healthy food was a surefire way to ensure strong bones and robust stamina.

She may not be able to protect me from puppy love, mononucleosis, getting cut from two high school sororities, and not making the cheerleading squad but, by God, I would be healthy.

It worked pretty well with my younger sister who, like my mom, wasn't a foodie. Unfortunately her formula didn't work so well with me. She wouldn't let me diet when I ballooned up. And she insisted mealtimes were for eating, even when I wasn't hungry.

So I rebelled in small ways. Every morning, while my mother was still asleep, I made myself two sunny-side-up eggs. I squished them with a fork until the yellows were splattered all over the plate. Tiptoeing to the downstairs bath, I flushed the gooey mess down the toilet. Carefully I put the plate with the remnants of the eggs prominently displayed in the sink and left the house fully satisfied and with an empty stomach.

And I only ate cherry pie for lunch and shunned the salads, entrees and veggie sides that were offered in seventh grade.

I'd show her.

Welcoming the Change

I welcome the change from being a director at work to being a patient at the treatment center. Someone is caring for me. Someone is monitoring me.

I relax the reins. It feels safe there. Contained. Warm and dusky. Like I imagine a womb.

I arrive at four p.m. on Monday, Tuesday and Thursday every week. We have different types of group therapy every day, plus individual therapy, with dinner in between. I learn to draw out the dinnertime routine. I spend fifteen minutes choosing my foods, getting my napkin and silverware, deciding on a drink, selecting my salad dressings. I have never experienced languishment in a meal setting and it soothes me.

I am acutely aware of the stretches of time between courses and the pauses after a few bites. I make conversation with the fellow "sufferer" I am sitting next to each night. I am aware of the staff's hovering presence. I engage them in conversation too sometimes.

Triggers and Needles

One spring evening, the group leader poses a question with seeming casualness.

"What are the triggers propelling you to abuse food?" she inquires. "To use it in other ways than the intended way—which is to nourish and sustain your body?"

"Hmmm," I wonder. "What propels me to head for the freezer for ice cream when I'm not even hungry?"

Quite surprisingly, the answer comes readily to me: *FRUSTRATION*.

"I get stuck. Or I stumble in an activity. Or I hit a temporary roadblock," I relate to the group. "And then, my mouth begins to salivate and immediately my mind swerves to what food I can eat—right this minute—to provide me with a reprieve from the discomfort enveloping me."

The therapist probes further. "What can you do to alter your automatic negative and destructive response to frustration?"

I'm thrown into neutral gear by that question. I stall. "I can't think what to do," I admit. "Except, of course, eat everything in sight. And then throw it all up. That soothes me."

It's clear to everyone in the group, including me, that I need to find other activities that calm me—that will induce a state of relaxation.

My immediate thoughts jump to knitting. You can't knit and binge at the same time. And as a wise knitter, Elizabeth Zimmerman, once quipped, "Knitting soothes the troubled spirit and it doesn't hurt the untroubled spirit either."

The next day, I dig out my knitting needles, balls of multicolored yarn and my stitch counter—stashed out of the way in the front hall closet under the stairs.

I started knitting in high school, mostly sweaters that didn't fit—too tight across the bust, too short for my broad hips.

When I had babies, it was small blankets and perky little booties and caps that I churned out. My sons were too young to balk at being adorned in handmade goodies with a few dropped stitches here and there.

When they each reached the discerning age when they could speak their mind (and it got younger and younger with each successive kid), they let me know in no uncertain terms that wearing a ski sweater knitted by their mother was at the top of the list of things weird second graders would do.

So I started on family room afghans, with an occasional scarf thrown in for variety. And my knitting needles clicked for many years.

I wonder why I ever stopped.

My Other Addiction

Throughout the years with ED, humor served as a mental mini-break from my anguish. As the days roll by, I am finding that displaying a sense of humor serves another purpose: it dispels my sense of separateness. When I tell a joke that someone else finds funny, there develops between us a bond. Aha—we both found the same joke funny.

It helps me find a comfortable place for myself, both inside and outside of the eating disordered group. A liberal use of humor lifts my spirits and lightens my load, while at the same time increasing camaraderie with those around me—a "we're in this together" attitude.

I read that humor reduces stress, put things in proper perspective, takes the edge off and helps us concentrate less on our disappointments, frustrations and woes. I am finding that true.

And a little gentlemen-bashing is not such a bad thing either.

Ten Wise Men

There were eleven people hanging onto a rope that came down from a helicopter. Ten were men and one was a woman. They all decided that one person should get off because if they didn't, the rope would break and everyone would die.

No one could decide who should go. Finally, the woman gave a really touching speech, saying how she would give up her life to save the others, because women were used to giving up things for their husbands and children, giving in to men and not receiving anything in return.

When she finished speaking, all the men started clapping.

The Power of the Sequence

An English professor wrote the words:

"A woman without her man is nothing" on the blackboard and directed his students to punctuate the sentence correctly.

The men wrote: "A woman, without her man, is nothing."

The women wrote, "A woman: without her, man is nothing."

Never underestimate the power of a woman.

My mood always lightens after finding new jokes. It's better than Prozac™, Xanax™, chardonnay and ED. No kidding.

Inner Accounting

During therapy, I give a lot of thought to why I spent so many years stepping on and off the scale; why I counted calories obsessively and critiqued my body flaws at every juncture.

And I stayed stuck, due to embarrassment about seeking help, as the bulimia continued unabated. I was ashamed—of the mindset that being a mature woman of a certain age, I should have known better.

Now I realize my incessant preoccupation with the nose of the scale kept me from focusing on other real life issues that called for thoughtful prodding. By keeping my focus on the scale, I didn't have to come to terms with the fact that my reproductive life was over or that I never would have a daughter. Who had the time for those ruminations? I was too busy perusing magazines and websites for the newest diet craze/program.

I didn't have to grow into my self—didn't have to face my lack of confidence and unfocused sense of my own essence. I didn't have to probe into why I felt unworthy. I didn't have to learn how to channel my anger into more appropriate behavior patterns. And I didn't have to tackle the field of conflict management.

As the years passed, I slowly became more accepting of my weight, my body image and my build. I became more comfortable in my own skin. As I succeeded professionally in myriad endeavors—sales, writing, broadcasting and speaking—my skills grew along with my self-confidence. I learned how to manage and make positive use of my conflicting emotions, tolerate ambivalence, embrace the "not neat and not tidy." And as my children, one by one, graduated from high school and left home to attend college, I realized I was a woman with valuable knowledge and life lessons to impart through my writing, radio interviewing and motivational speaking.

Something New: Intuitive Eating

The fashionable ideal, as portrayed by media stars, fashion models and beauty contest winners, over the years has changed from the Lillian Russell/Marilyn Monroe standard, which was frankly female and curvaceous, to the Jane Fonda/Candice Bergen standard, which is Unisex Slim.

Miss Sweden of 1951 was five-foot-seven and weighed 151 pounds; Miss Sweden of 1983, she was five-nine and weighed just 109 pounds! Betty Cantrell, Miss America 2016, is five-foot-seven and is as slim as my index finger.

The concern for fashion and the determination to try and attain an unrealistic body type have turned many women into chronic dieters.

I can relate.

Do our genes determine the size of our jeans?

Different people can eat identical meals and some will gain more weight than others. Some people tend to store unneeded calories as fat; others lay them down as muscle. Studies published in the *New England Journal of Medicine* contain the strongest evidence to date that the genes a person inherits are the dominant factor determining whether that person is fat, lean or in between.

I can relate. (Genetically doomed. Thanks, Dad.)

Is thin still in? Apparently. In April 1994, Rosie Daley, the personal chef responsible for helping Oprah Winfrey lose seventy-two pounds in just eight months, published a low-salt, low-fat, low-sugar cookbook. Oprah swears Rosie's recipes for such things as mock Caesar Salad and unfried French fries changed her life. (It certainly changed Rosie's!)

In The Kitchen with Rosie: Oprah's Favorite Recipes rang up 1.4 million sales even BEFORE its official publication date. Barnes & Noble sold 20,000 copies in a single day. Booksellers were scurrying to keep it on the shelves and people everywhere were trying out the new recipes in their own kitchens nightly.

I can relate.

Alas, as Oprah confided in 2016, the battle of her bulge continues. She has now bought into Weight Watchers, and thinks *that* is the perfect weight loss plan, as thus far she has lost over thirty pounds.

And at this juncture, there's still a plethora of weight-related books sitting on bookstore shelves, keeping company with Rosie's:

Cavewomen Don't Get Fat: The Paleo Chic Diet for Rapid Results
The Alkaline Diet Plan
The Carb Lovers Diet
The 20/20 Diet
Trim Healthy Mama Plan
The 10 Day Green Smoothie Cleanse
The Ketogenic Diet

Waiting for eager and hopeful purchasers.

I can relate.

I am facing it:

Weight lost tends to creep back on.

Portions increase.

Snacks multiply.

A bite becomes a sliver. A sliver becomes a slice.

Time between weigh-ins lengthens.

Exercise is not quite so vigorous—or frequent.

Nonfat leads to low-fat leads to ice cream.

Alas, the cause is not lost.

There is one more concept to embrace: Intuitive Eating.

Intuitive Eating? No "Weigh"

Intuitive eating?

No "weigh." That's crazy.

After bingeing and purging for forty-six years, the whole concept is totally foreign to me.

I am utterly and totally lacking any intuitiveness in relation to what foods I like and don't like. I have an ingrained "forbidden foods" mentality and I habitually spend hours and hours chasing after the latest diet fad.

The concept of portion control?

Ha.

A bulimic eats until ready to burst. There is no perception of "comfortably full."

Intuitive eating? What a joke.

I resent the outlay of money for the book and very reluctantly begin reading, with great skepticism, I might add.

Here's the concept: Eating what you want and not gaining weight. I certainly get that mindset. Bulimics are masters of that.

I skim the book's content, already discouraged and despairing. There is simply no possible way I can ever hope to have a safe relationship with food. There is simply no possible way I can put dieting on the back burner.

Hacking Back to the Main Trail

I tried the Cottage Cheese and the Graham Cracker diets in my preteens. Capricious experiments with the Atkins Diet, the Zone Diet, the South Beach Diet and the Raw Food Diet followed. Battling the bulge became my *raison d'être*. The Skinny Bitch Diet was the last plan I tried to follow. I certainly didn't become skinny, but I did become a super, raving, and very hungry bitch.

I am not alone. According to the U.S. Weight Loss Market: 2014 Status Report & Forecast, the weight-loss industry is a $60.5 billion a year industry.

I guess I am not the only one trying to satisfy my longing for a vanilla malt by drinking eight glasses of lemon-flavored Crystal Light a day. I guess I am not the only one trying to banish the delectable, mouth-watering image of a good old-fashioned grilled cheese sandwich on white bread—oozing butter—from my consciousness. Trying to squash down the desire for this goody by gnawing on a bag of raw carrots or two low-fat mozzarella cheese sticks simply does not work. Eating the damn sandwich, butter and all, is the action that vanquishes that desire.

Setting myself on a carefully planned and faultlessly executed course of eating and drinking did not work. Planning the kind and amount of food I should eat didn't yield lasting results either.

I continued the binge/purge cycle. I continued the visceral pursuit of leanness. I continued losing the battle of the bulge. And most importantly, though I didn't realize it at the time, I kept reading *Intuitive Eating* by Elyse Resch.

I learned that intuitive eating is really just about normal eating—normal eating that can lead to developing a safe relationship with both food and with my own body.

Shocking.

I learned that intense eating is a normal response to dieting. Anguishing over each morsel of food and perpetually restricting calories and carbs ensures we are in a chronic dieting state. Eating unconsciously with little regard for true physical hunger and using food to cope with emotions only sabotages attempts to force the needle of the scale in a southward direction.

What do the naturally intuitive eaters do that I don't do?

They keep their bodies fed biologically with adequate energy and carbs so a primal desire to overeat is not triggered.

They give themselves permission to eat so that intense feelings of deprivation don't build up.

They take away the value judgment of good and bad as it relates to food intake. They banish the "I'm good if I eat under 1,000 calories a day and I'm bad if I don't" mantra.

They pause while eating—listening to their bodies so they can tell when they are comfortably full. They don't push away from the dinner table feeling stuffed, disgusted with themselves for not resisting that second helping of mashed potatoes.

They find pleasure and satisfaction in the eating experience. They savor it, not fear it.

They find other ways to comfort themselves that do not involve food, when feeling lonely, anxious, frustrated or angry. They don't mindlessly open the door of the refrigerator seeking solace.

They accept their unique genetic blueprint, instead of tirelessly trying to squeeze into skirts two sizes smaller than their frame can naturally accommodate.

"Intuitive eaters," Resch says, "are unaffected eaters. They eat whatever they choose, while marching to their own inner hunger signals."

I am beginning to get it, but it's still pretty scary to me. It will involve change. Change of routine and change of mindset. Giving up habits dating back to a time before boobs and braces. How would I know what to eat and not eat, if I didn't have a template?

I began by placing my trust in Resch, who cites that well-intentioned, "healthy" meal plans were not helping people maintain permanent weight control.

With trepidation and mild skepticism, I tentatively embark on the intuitive eating journey. What did I have to lose?

Favorite Food

One of the first exercises *Intuitive Eating* suggests is to make a list of your favorite foods. For someone so food obsessed, it seems strange that this was such a tough assignment for me, but it was.

I had spent my entire adult life eating all kinds of indulgent foods. I didn't have to be too discerning because I always ate with the knowledge that I would be throwing it all up. There was no need to choose between a Heath bar and a Baby Ruth. I could have them both.

"Hmmm," I wondered, "knowing now that whatever I ate I would have to digest without the purging bypass, I guess I need to be a tad more discriminating and introspective regarding my choices."

Unbelievably it took me three weeks to come up with five things:
- Pecan pie
- Three Musketeers bar
- Vanilla malt with extra malt powder
- Crusty mac and cheese
- Sweet potato fries

I was immediately horrified to find out that if you want to rid yourself of an obsession with a certain food, eat it and only it for three straight days—that should cure you of your obsession.

I balked, like a battering cow being led to slaughter. I sensed disaster and stubbornly refused to advance.

Splendor in the Grass

I never mourned my losses, defeats or humiliations, my divorce and the deaths of loved ones, the disappointments and dashed dreams.

I never pared down the too-high expectations I held that were impossible to meet.

I never had to.

I vomited all my tears, sadness, and torn and ragged feelings into the toilet. And it provided short-term, albeit artificial, relief. A temporary respite from uncomfortable and unwelcome emotions.

Now that I choose to abandon that brand of self-medication, I need new tools to help me reconcile myself to the losses I previously stuffed down and rid myself of—without fully understanding, without working through, without puzzling it out, without reaching mindful resolution.

Words soothe me.

I cleave to the poem "Splendour in the Grass" by William Wordsworth. It provides me with a clue to dealing with the past:

> *Though nothing can bring back the hour*
> *Of splendour in the grass, of glory in the flower;*
> *We will grieve not, rather find*
> *Strength in what remains behind.*

Books calm me.

I turn to *Necessary Losses* by Judith Viorst. It offers me a template within which to craft my future.

Viorst writes that everyone, of course, has losses and the way we handle our losses marks the way we get through life. Coping with loss and replacing what we have lost with other things makes the loss more palatable.

I think of the day, years ago, that I watched one of my sons umpire his first Little League baseball game.

That morning, as I plugged in the coffee pot, I recalled past stories of rude coaches, irate parents and jeering spectators yelling at teenage umpires. My husband once saw a young umpire reduced to tears and mumbles by cruel bystanders harassing his every call, arguing over every play. So I decided to go to the game. Certainly if there was a chance—no matter how remote—that the coaches wouldn't protect him, the parents wouldn't shield him, and the players might ridicule him, I needed to be there to anchor him, root for him and see him through. Isn't that my role as his mother?

I watch my son ump his first game. I catch a few random grumbles from parents in the stands when my son calls the batter safe at first base. I watch the veteran umpire confer intensely with my son after he calls a player out at home plate. Watching him that bright spring morning, standing behind home plate calling the pitches in a decisive voice and holding to his call even when challenged, makes me realize that he has matured. I know that he has reached a point in his development where he is able to tolerate name calling, challenges to his decisions and adversarial positions—without the protection of his mother's hovering presence. On that dusty baseball field, his childhood was sliding away and a promising, self-confident, young man was emerging.

That realization made the loss of his dependence on me, and my powerlessness to protect him and shield him any longer, easier to bear. And it reinforced my pride in raising a self-empowered son who, when entering college the following fall, would have the tools to adjust and persevere.

I am on the brink of escape from the bulimic's distorted mind. I am beginning to recognize that relinquishing our losses—beginning with our connection to our own mothers and extending past the loss of intimate connections to our own children—leads to healthier self-image and identity. I am ready to embrace the losses so I can also fully celebrate new milestones and triumphs.

"Losing is the price we pay for living," says Judith Viorst.

And I am ready to live.

Selling Yoga

My friend Joy sold me on the benefits of yoga, not because she was such a whiz at the practice of it or knew the best yoga instructors in the neighborhood. Nor did she have the inside track on which yoga works best for an aging baby boomer body, be it Ashtanga, Hatha, Power, Bikram, Restorative, Hot or Yin.

Nope, Joy sold me on yoga because, at age seventy, through the practice of yoga, she was able to begin the process of eradicating bulimia from her life.

Here's what I learned:

- Yoga creates inner shifts.
- Yoga gives us the strength and insight to navigate these changes.
- Yoga won't keep us from being scared or confused or overwhelmed, but it can guide us so we don't get lost in our feelings, or jump impulsively and short-circuit the whole healing process.
- Yoga facilitates the action of internally motivated choices becoming a reality.

My awareness heightened, I register for my first yoga class.

I look around at my fellow practitioners. As they stretch and warm up, the instructor lights five scented candles and flips a switch that floods the high-ceilinged room with soft background music. Strains of disjointed conversations swirl around me. A woman nearby refers to a bout of breast cancer. A gentleman leaning against the back wall mentions just being relieved of his duties at a local accounting firm. Clearly, I am not the only one who is dealing with change—scary change. As I learn Downward Facing Dog, Cobra and Reclining Twist, I wonder:

What else can we do when chaos descends and confusion whirls around us? We all seem to be seeking answers.

I head home. And while cutting up fresh cauliflower to roast, I recall the wartime quote from Winston Churchill, British prime minister during the darkest hours of World War II. "If you're going through hell, keep going."

Geoff Loftus, a *Forbes* contributor who writes about history and pop cultures, says, "Churchill used language to rouse the fighting spirit he believed was still alive in the British people, saying, 'If you're going through hell, keep going.' And the line that summed up his personal career and the spirit that led the British people to victory: 'Never, never, never give up.'

"In other words, his plan for success: Complete and total defiance."

I decide that that is how I will keep going too. I will defy my demons while figuring out how to move successfully forward.

The first thing I do is register for more yoga classes.

Affirming the Affirmative

I begin turning inward.

Dealing with my demons demands a change in tactics, behavior and mindset. I start out small. I begin punctuating this new phase in my road to recovery by daily citing affirmations before I even rise out of my bed in the morning. Affirmations propel forward movement, bringing the goal of living an uncluttered, simpler life that much closer to reality. Affirmations bring direction, clarify and help verbalize goals and aspirations, and help free us from the constraints of compulsive, mindless actions that are destructive to our healing and recovery.

Here are some of my affirmations:
- I view each hurdle as an opportunity to grow.
- I am banishing the negative and embracing the positive.

- I am stepping out of my comfort zone so that I can be the best I can be.
- Each day I am getting stronger, more mindful and more resolute.
- I am listening to my body and recognizing triggers that set off binges and purges.
- I am continuing to calm my spirit and anchor myself in tranquility.

Heeding these affirmations and reciting them each day also propels me to take actions to prevent a lapse into the bulimic nightmare. I start with mini-steps.

I begin purging my pantry of tempting foods. The first week, I can hardly throw out any tempting morsels, but I do manage to get rid of a half-eaten box of caramel popcorn and the stash of stale Halloween candy. The next week I tackle the cereal boxes—the first to get the heave-ho is Frosted Flakes. Those sugar-coated goodies have been a life-long nemesis. Purging the pantry is becoming enjoyable. Soon I rid the shelves of the boxes and boxes of instant pudding—too tempting to whip up when my freezer is bare of ice cream. In the matter of a month, my shelves are stripped clean of foods that offer temptation and can arouse the sleeping demons.

I learn to rest when I am tired, not forage the kitchen in an attempt to boost my energy level with calorie-laden goodies. I learn to eat before I am ravenous and to stop eating before I am uncomfortably full. I begin to pause between bites of my dinner and employ my senses to see the colors of the food I am eating, to feel the textures, to smell the aromas. It's a slow process—this instituting of good habits—but I doggedly pursue it nonetheless.

Sustained effort is my aim and I vow not to get unnecessarily depressed by setbacks and reversals. I keep in mind the steps I have to take to get to where I want to be. I accept there will be times when I feel irritable and discouraged, but I am adapting a warrior mentality to ward off the "I don't have what it takes" attitude that will only lead to dead ends and defeat.

I recognize early in this process that I must piece together a way to deal with my discomfort. I am abandoning the old model of anesthetizing my discomfort with mindless gorging. But in order to stay in the present with myself and my feelings, I need to develop an effective antidote to dissipate my distress. My aim is to stay in the moment when the discomfort descends, to move into—not away from—it.

I recall a recent flight I had taken, when the plane was wracked with turbulence. One of the stewardesses, on her way to grab a seat, dipped her head and looked me square in the face. "Release your grip on the sides of the seat," she gently admonished me. "Relax your body and move with the plane's flow. Don't go rigid and don't brace yourself."

Ah. The old "Try and Be Present" mantra. Feel the anxiety and, yoga-like, imagine it flowing away from you, naturally and steadily.

I keep it up. Remembering to let go—again and again and again—when discomfort comes calling. It's a navigational device to affect change and a recognition that old habits may be familiarly comforting but don't yield the results I so desire.

I may be taking mouse steps every day, but they add up to giant steps in the long run.

Bulik on Therapy

I search YouTube for videos on bulimia and, of course, the local bookstore for books.

I am not disappointed. There are hundreds of videos and books on the binge-and-purge topic.

One video catches my attention immediately. It is an interview clip with Dr. Cynthia Bulik, which originally aired on *CBS This Morning* in 2012. She initiates the interview by focusing on a body image survey involving 1,900 women age fifty and above. Here are the findings:

- Thirteen percent have an eating disorder
- Eight percent purge
- Sixty-two percent said weight negatively impacts their life

Dr. Bulik is the director of the University of North Carolina Center of Excellence for Eating Disorders. She explained these statistics by saying there is great pressure on older women today, as everything is about looking younger or trying to stay thin, which leads to unhealthy eating.

I was immediately intrigued and ordered her book, *Midlife Eating Disorders: Your Journey to Recovery*. Drawing from both sources, here are some tidbits that resonated with me:

There are three patterns to eating disorders in older women: Some had an eating disorder in adolescence and got better, only to relapse in later life. Some are chronic eating-disordered women. Some develop an eating disorder for the first time in later life.

"It's a cradle-to-grave ball and chain," Dr. Bulik states.

After affirming that eating disorders do have genetic and biological components, Dr. Bulik cited some triggers:

- Divorce
- Pressure not to age
- Loss
- Death of loved ones
- Empty nest or kids boomeranging back

And, from informally talking to both friends and acquaintances, here are a few more stress factors emerging in midlife that can catapult us into bingeing and purging:

- Dating
- Career difficulties
- Emotional and physiological changes occurring during menopause
- Caregiving
- Isolation
- Financial constraints

"There's no niche for grandmas anymore," Dr. Bulik further elaborates. But one thing women fifty and older can do is "get out of the appearance focus." When you look in the mirror, don't focus on your body flaws. Say something positive about yourself, not related to how you look.

Dr. Bulik feels there are many reasons women over fifty don't seek treatment. One is the embarrassment and shame factor—the feeling they should have outgrown it. Additionally, Dr. Bulik cited the myriad of responsibilities and obstacles to seeking treatment, such as caregiving and full-time jobs.

Emphasizing that all recoveries are unique, Dr. Bulik does offer some general observations:

Bulimics are ambivalent about entering therapy because their bulimia does serve a function, such as controlling their weight and managing anxiety. This needs to be recognized.

A less direct approach to therapy, characterized by rolling with the resistance and focusing on smaller victories, should be employed, rather than harsher therapy that Bulik characterizes as "sending a battering ram through closed doors."

Patients should be encouraged to introduce a welcoming, non-judgmental, compassionate spirituality into their lives, which can lead to more gracious attitudes towards themselves.

Patients should be encouraged to build honest and authentic friendships, because, as one former bulimic observes, "people with eating disorders live in an emotional bubble wrap."

Bulimics should be helped to make a conscious choice to choose happiness—dropping the mantle of entitlement—and to look for ways to experience pleasure and joy.

I am beginning to get it. The therapy I am receiving—cognitive behavior therapy (CBT)—is helping me forgive myself for my shortcomings. It is helping me to meet my own needs in the same way that I so willingly meet the needs of others. It is teaching me to give myself the gift of time to recover, to practice self-compassion and to take appropriate risks. It is helping me understand that I am stronger than I thought and that I do have the power to change, to become more engaged in the world and in my relationships. It is possible for me to imagine succeeding at banishing my demons. By regarding my mental pain as fleeting and impermanent—not something I am doomed to feel forever—I can soldier on. I can continue to strive to be the brave warrior I have always wanted to be.

I can do it.

Flaws

Over time, I began to realize that my family—particularly my sons and husband—loved me not for my "perfection" but in spite of my flaws. It was quite a freeing realization.

Visiting the Land of the Yearning

I once again visit my children and grandchildren in New York and we all go out to dinner at a neighborhood Italian eatery. To my utter surprise, I leave half my pasta dish uneaten. I have never done that before, especially when I visit the Land of the Yearning—my moniker for where my children physically reside.

A few days later, I return to orange trees and sunshine. At group, the leader casually announces that it's the nutritionist's birthday and there's chocolate cake.

"Who would like a slice?" she asks. Three in the group decline. Tanya and I accept. I greedily delve in, quickly shoveling in the mounds of icing with bits of cake (I have always been a sucker for icing).

Surprisingly, after about ten bites I am able to pause and gauge my hunger level. I feel content. I put down my fork. And push the plate away from my body.

A new feeling washes over me: satiety without gluttony.

Musings

My mother did not breastfeed. And my mother always boasts that she weaned me off the bottle at a very early age in my life. I wonder if that is why my most favorite comfort food in the world, barring none, is an extra-large vanilla malt with extra malt powder?

It doesn't take psychiatric training to figure out that one: Big. White. Sweet. Liquid. That you suck to get.

I find a substitute, if not for the tit, then for the malt:

Chobani Greek Yogurt, pineapple flavored, enhanced with one packet of Truvia. Eaten at room temperature. Slurped up with a plastic spoon.

An Ending

It's April 30, 2012 and tomorrow is my last day in the intensive outpatient program (IOP).

Here's a bare-bones description of our unvarying routine:

We meet three days a week from four p.m. to seven p.m.

One day a week is devoted to art therapy.

One session a week centers on nutrition.

Each day, a different therapist sees us as a group and then sees each of us alone for fifteen minutes.

Each evening, all the patients and staff eat dinner together.

At first, I find the group wildly interesting and listen, spellbound, to each participant's story. Alcohol abuse. Victim of domestic violence. Cutting. Snorting. Starving. And of course, bingeing and purging.

We seem to be thrown-together strangers, riding the turbulent waves on a battered ship. And though we long for the shore, our shipmates provide solace and company.

As the weeks pass, the "Group" makeup changes, but the fabric of the stories remains the same: addiction-saddled individuals riddled with angst, desperation, helplessness and depression. In varying degrees, it seems we are all trying to make headway in kicking whatever "habit" we have in order to take back the reins of our lives.

My six-week stint takes longer than planned due to my heavy work schedule, an out-of-state conference, and out-of-town family events.

I begin to notice the subtle changes in my attitude toward the other participants. I am getting impatient with some of them—frustrated by their lack of progress. Suspicious that maybe for some, therapy is a way of avoiding life, hiding out in the safety zone of their illness. The needle on my empathy meter is hovering on empty and I know in my heart it is time for me to depart.

But yet, as the time for leave-taking draws near, I also realize I am going to miss my group. I am going to miss the atmosphere of trust— the enveloping feeling that with these people I don't have to hide my eating issues. I don't have to be Miss Perfect, the master of coping. Only when I pull into the eating disorder clinic do I feel that I am handing over the reins to a force stronger than myself—a force that will nurture me back to health. It's been a long time since I have had that kind of feeling. And, I wonder, if once I leave this place, will I be able to duplicate the canopy of caretaking and create that for myself?

But tonight—my last night—I put my concerns aside. It will be a leaning-forward moment, not a sitting-back moment. It will be a time to soak up every last bit of wisdom, strength, confidence and resoluteness I can from every session, every leader, every participant. To hug and cry and smile, and walk away with greater mindfulness and renewed hope of continued success.

Part Three: Re-Engagement

Sometimes you can only find Heaven by
slowly backing away from Hell.
—Carrie Fisher

Introduction

It's a funny thing. We get so bogged down in satisfying ourselves in the moment—watching that new movie on Netflix or running out to buy the moisturizer that *Glamour* magazine touts as the must-have for youthful dewiness—that we may not be doing the things that will be best for us in the long run. Those things which will give our life meaning.

As the days and months progress after treatment, the fear of missing out (FOMO) begins to subside and I naturally find more time to practice a type of holistic productivity. It's productivity born out of thoughtful focus, more deliberate parsing of my life goals, and a less distractible frame of mind.

These months post-professional treatment will be filled with unbridled energy to forge new ties. I will ponder things I have never pondered. I will re-engage with gusto. But I will also recognize the vestiges of disordered eating still clinging to my bootstraps. And I will suffer loss anew.

After all the progress I have made in eradicating ED, a self-stigmatizing mindset will still pervade my universe. I hate fat. I can't tolerate being fat. And if I don't find a way to get rid of this fat...well, I don't even want to consider the actions I will take.

Gradually, I find my way through the mist. In ways that even surprised me.

Fertilizing, Cultivating and Preserving My Bloom

With the passing years, bulimia wielded its own evil power. Spread its poisonous tentacles. Gradually, without alarming notice, I began to withdraw and retreat from meaningful and truthful interactions. My thinking shifted and I became convinced that face-to-face interactions weren't that important. I embraced the belief that true personal growth can only be attained by slogging it out in solitude.

That was, until I discovered psychiatrist Daniel J. Siegel. His position on optimal health and well-being alters all my faulty assumptions. Siegel is an internationally acclaimed author, psychiatrist, and award–winning educator who deals in practical application to enhance well-being. Siegel says three things shape us: relationships, the mind, and the body. In his groundbreaking book, *The Neurobiology of We*, he writes, "…the mind actually emerges out of the interaction between your brain and your relationships." Siegel refers to this triad as the key to moving you from stress to equanimity, transforming trauma and living mindfully.

It's beginning to make sense to me. I am shedding the moniker of a bulimic. I am slipping off the harness of shame and guilt. Gradually, I'm breaking through my own armor of solitude. I am no longer spending hours alone—squandering time, wallowing in mediocrity or drowning in remorse. I am moving out of my own stuck way.

Energy washes over me. I begin to cultivate new friendships—make plans to develop my own street gang. I interconnect with those I find engaging and admirable and provocative. I lay the foundation for planning new initiatives, exploring options, seeking out opportunities.

I discover paths that naturally lead to creating communities where once there were none.

Create community. Its simple alliteration lures me.

I approach a friend who, like me, is enamored with the printed page. Together we explore the possibility of starting a monthly book club. Sounds pretty doable. Replicable. Easy to implement. We begin.

Immediately our efforts are bogged down by a dilemma. Do we invite our buddies, some who aren't even interested in books, but would be hurt if left out? Or do we take a bold leap and only invite women who are ardent readers, but not necessarily friends? We choose the latter course.

We are barraged by angry females gnashing their teeth over the exclusion. We hold our ground, staying true to our core mission. "It's not about friendship," we reiterate. "It's about literature: reading it, talking about it, loving it."

And, though not entirely true, we plead the case that we will be delving into lofty, non-commercial fiction and non-fiction requiring ample time, concentration and perspiration. Most of them back down and happily go back to playing Canasta and perusing the mall. (Wow— that last sentence smacks of cattiness! Am I emerging as a self–serving bitch or what?)

Collapsing Into a Craving

I hurriedly stuff caramels into my mouth. The same caramels I bought weeks ago. The same caramels that never before had posed a threat to my "no binge" resolve—because hey, they just weren't "my thing."

As always, the caramels rest in the cut-glass crystal bowl—the one I regularly passed on my way to turn on the TV. The one I was now frantically digging my fingers into, pulling out handfuls of caramels, unwrapping them as fast as I could, and heedlessly popping them into my mouth.

Where was the pride I felt only this morning when I noticed the bowl was still filled to the brim with those butterscotch-colored wonders?

That is why this sudden turn of events is utterly terrifying. Only the night before, I was busy jotting down random observations for the upcoming book I hope to publish on my successful battle with bulimia. And now I am once again enveloped in a whirling, jolting lack of self-control.

WTF?

I stuff more caramels down my throat in an effort to ward off such disturbing thoughts. I do not pause to savor the velvety sweetness as the caramels make contact with my salivating mouth. I propel myself into the empty kitchen and, with even greater force of movement, pop handful after handful of bite-size licorice bits into my mouth too.

I go back for more caramels. The bowl is empty. I'm numb, but not nearly numb enough to stop the fear from coursing through my veins. Is that what a relapse feels like? Like a bull charging a concrete wall—courting disaster?

I groan.

"It's only a mini binge at this point," I try to reassure myself. "I can stop before I inflict real harm."

I circle the kitchen island again and again, resisting the licorice. My breathing slows in response to the rhythmic, repetitive looping movements. I am beginning to shed the numbness. I blink and become more aware of the time, the bright lights, my sweating brow, and my racing heart. That familiar feeling of acute fullness is there—more full than I am comfortable with, but not bursting-full.

I clench my hands together. I draw deep, ragged breaths. I stop mindlessly grabbing for anything sweet in sight.

I wonder if things had gone differently had I been able to stay in the moment and slowly savor each caramel square and each morsel of black licorice? Would I have been able to stop myself from mindlessly stuffing the candy in my mouth? How many pieces of candy would it have taken to satisfy my hunger, subdue the craving and vanquish ED-like behavior once more if I had followed the therapy template to slow down and savor?

I'm left pondering, but not purging.

Bulimic Jew or Jewish Bulimic?

I am a Reform Jew, not an Orthodox one.

I was consecrated at age six when I started Sunday School. I got to wear my shiny, black patent leather Mary Janes for the very first time.

I was not privy to a Bat Mitzvah. It was okay by me. Hebrew school was an opportunity to closely study the boys, not learn the *aleph* and *bet*.

I was confirmed in tenth grade. I remember my dress being too tight and my bosom way too prominent. And the presence of all those home-baked pastries in the reception hall only heightened my discomfort.

I wasn't the only one of my Jewish friends suffering pangs of remorse over an inherited full-figured body. The ideal stature—tall and lanky, willowy and long-waisted—was simply not realistically attainable. We all were relatively short, curvy, and full-busted. Jewish holidays revolved around food; our culture celebrated mealtimes as sacrosanct. And we were constantly bombarded by kugel, mouth-watering brisket and the plaintive pleading of our grandmothers to "Eat, *bubbeleh*, eat."

"Judaism supports the notion that our bodies are sacred," Rabbi Sara Hurwitz stated in *The Forward* a number of years ago. I had never thought of my body in that way. My physical being was always the font of unacceptable urges, uncontrollable appetites, unrelenting displeasure.

"The body is the soul's house," she further affirmed.

"Wow," I realized, "my inner house was anything but hallowed and revered. It was in total disarray—the direct opposite of my physical home, which was always clean and orderly and well appointed." I couldn't tolerate it any other way.

It was no wonder my life lacked spiritual nourishment. I was obsessed with the number registering every morning on my scale. It was my mood barometer, the benchmark for my outlook and attitude for the next twenty-four hours—until I stepped on that mood-defining mechanism once again. It was no wonder I had no energy left over to deal with my unacceptable feelings of anger, resentment, jealousy, and insecurity. I didn't have to face my uncomfortable inner turmoil because food-related behaviors occupied my mind entirely.

I threw away my scale. Then I utilized a less precise way to gauge my poundage—the prominence of my cheekbones and the fit of my brown skirt with the white polka dots. Soon I grew weary of those measures of my worth, too. I yearned for something less quantifiable and more substantive.

"What," I wondered, "would be a worthy addition in my quest for authentic wholeness?"

I looked to Judaism.

It was a natural progression for me, as I was working in the Jewish communal world. First I was the managing editor of our town's Jewish newspaper (my most favorite job in the world). When my husband and I relocated south, I went to work at a Conservative synagogue and then later at the Jewish Federation. Marketing and programming were my forte, so researching new subjects and time-honored rituals was a natural off-shoot of my job.

Instead of stepping on the scale, or continuously studying my reflection and lamenting what I didn't have—a skinny-ass body—I began to embrace the art of gratitude, being thankful for the gift of my imperfect body itself. I started reciting the *Modeh Ani* each morning upon arising. First in Hebrew, then in English.

Modeh ani lefaneicha melech chai v'kayam shehechezarta binishmati bechemlah—rabbah enumatecha.

I gratefully thank you, O living and eternal King, for You have returned my soul within me with compassion—abundant is Your faithfulness.

And over time, I modified it by adding this: *And please turn on my spiritual electricity so that I can be the best I can be. Amen.*

I began investigating Jewish rituals. And I discovered the celebration of Rosh Chodesh, a Jewish holiday marking the passage of the new moon. It is also called the day of good beginnings—not the day of new beginnings. Rosh Chodesh is an opportunity through prayer, song, and gathering with other women to reflect on the previous month and the new month to be.

The moon's unfailing re-appearance after every disappearance became identified in my mind with rebirth after every setback, renewal after every failed effort. Celebrating the emergence of the new moon helped remove barriers that were blocking me and heightened awareness of what constricted me. Not only the scale. I was boxed in by how narrowly I defined my beauty and worth. I looked in the mirror. When cheekbones were prominent, all was sparkling. When stripped of this vestige of thinness, I became demoralized and depressed—out of touch with my talents, strengths and uniqueness. Rosh Chodesh helped me utilize my inextinguishable spark of optimism. I gained an awareness of forces I could call on to wean me away from the endless cycle of pounds gained, pounds lost, pounds regained and pounds lost again.

Prayer, in any religion, helps connect with healing energy. And for me, while battling bulimia, praying for both others and myself became a daily source of ritualized soothing. The haunting melody of the *Mi Sheberakh* first came to my attention while listening to a recording by the late Debbie Friedman. Here's an excerpt, in English:

May the source of strength Who blessed the ones before us Help us find the courage To make our lives a blessing, And let us say Amen.

Though I was not a student of *Kabbalah* (Jewish mysticism), the concept of shattered sparks—of retrieving those parts of us that were lost—resonated strongly with me. For instance, I had never simply savored a bowl of ice cream. Why bother savoring a small portion when I could zone out, devour the entire gallon as fast as I could, and then cheat the scale by throwing it all up minutes later?

So, I started by putting only one scoop of ice cream in a bowl and, as I began to eat mindfully, setting my spoon down between each tasting. I savored the chocolate chips. I delighted in the creamy smoothness of the ice cream itself. I noticed its contrasts of color.

Could enjoying food for food's sake itself be rekindled? As Rabbi Nachman of Breslov said, "As long as a tiny flame remains, a great fire can be rekindled." I took that to mean that if I could enjoy a small bowl of ice cream, maybe I could relearn the pleasure of focused eating, of intuitive eating, of eating when I was physically hungry—not frustrated or bored. Maybe I could truly feel full after a reasonable intake of food. And maybe I could truly enjoy the process. I started to believe that my shattered sparks could become a path to healing and wholeness.

Another Jewish concept that helped me greatly in my struggles was the practice of *Selichot*—of asking forgiveness for those we have harmed. Not surprisingly, the person I had harmed the most was me. It wasn't easy to let go of the idealized version of myself as the ultimate fixer, the ultimate coping machine, the ultimate bastion of strength and serenity. To shed the mistaken belief that everyone else needed advice and help, but not me, was a daunting challenge. I had to be the strong one. The glue. The hub. If I wasn't that person, then who was I?

I started forgiving myself for harboring resentments, mismanaging my anger, internalizing my despair, and for not being perfect. I put down the heavy load of crap I had been figuratively dragging in a knapsack behind me. I asked for help. And when I didn't get what I felt I needed, I asked again. I drew strength from that help. And I began to mend.

My physical house now is less regimented, more unprompted and ever-evolving. I use my gigantic dining room table as a receptacle to hold all my projects in various stages of completion. I welcome the pile of gym shoes on the stairs—reminding me of my recent walks along the bay. I look lovingly on the haphazard piles of books in every room—delighting in the knowledge and adventure eventual reading will impart to me.

My spiritual house inside my newly cherished body now is less regimented, more unprompted and ever-evolving too. I revel in the intervals, not the completions. The undone, not the neat and tidy faux finish. The moments. Not the long haul. The sustenance. Not the binges. The serenity. Not the purges.

A bulimic Jew or a Jewish bulimic?

Does it really matter?

Not any more.

Resisting the Pull of the Other

I am resisting the pull of "The Other."
- Boot camp-like workouts that promise to re-shape my body
- Invasive surgery that promises ageless skin
- Makeup routine that demands unreasonable time and expense
- A regimen reflecting worship of a culture of youth

I am embracing the pull of "The Self."
- To be authentic
- To cultivate a healthy mind, body and spirit
- To celebrate my imperfect uniqueness
- To hold close my dreams and passions
- To revel in the gift of good friends and loving family
- To putter with wild abandon

Puttering

Webster's Encyclopedic Unabridged Dictionary of the English Language defines the verb "putter" as "to busy or occupy oneself in an ineffective manner." Ineffective, in this case, means not producing results.

When I think of puttering, I conjure up the image of a relaxed person sort of aimlessly wandering around the house doing little incidental, mindless activities that may or may not need to be done at that moment, but that just feel good to be doing at that particular time.

Puttering, to me, is spending the morning at home, wiping off the dust on the leaves of my philodendron plant, rearranging the family photos on top of my armoire, reading the editorial page in the newspaper, and savoring a second cup of freshly brewed coffee while really listening to my Pandora selections on my iPhone.

Puttering is doing things that, if they aren't accomplished, won't really be missed, but if they are done, lend peace of mind and a sense of pleasure to the person who did them.

Puttering is NOT something I was capable of pulling off for most of my adult life. Puttering is not doable when you are leading a life dictated by an eating disorder. How do you putter around when all you are thinking of is what you can eat, should you eat, when can you eat, and how fast after you do eat can you throw it all up?

Puttering, for me, was an elusive art.

Puttering—staying at home to wander through my rooms on a wet, stormy morning in July, enjoying the solitude, appreciating the greenery seen from every window, admiring my grandmother's delicate antique cups and saucers in the breakfront—was an oddity in my constricted world.

Lately, I find myself leisurely roaming the rooms of my house, filling my mind with pleasant thoughts, and busying my fingers with mundane, marginal activities that are not needed, demanded nor of immediate concern.

If it's not urgent, I don't do it.

If it's not needed, I let it go.

If it's not necessary, I put it off.

The art of puttering.

I am beginning to love it so.

A New Kind of Bingeing

I have now watched eighty-five out of 100 posted episodes of *Grey's Anatomy*.

Teeny, tiny flickers of anxiety are flaring up. What will I do with those dangerous evening hours once I've exhausted the accessible episodes?

Gleefully, I learn that forty-five more episodes of Grey's Anatomy have just been made available for home viewing.

Whew.

Heavier? Lighter? The Same?

It's been forty-six hours since the termination of my outpatient therapy at the treatment center. I feel rudderless. Restless. It's a combination of losing both acceptability and accountability at the same time.

I make the decision to continue in private therapy once a week for the time being. It proves to be not as satisfying and engaging as the group, but provides a transition I sorely need.

Because...the trusty polka dot skirt has gotten tighter. And I am upset.

Released from the program's strictures, I can weigh myself anytime I desire. I can abandon the intuitive eating template. And I can fully indulge my chronic dieting habit.

So, along with my reduced therapy sessions, I fall back into a familiar pattern of incessantly exploring weight-loss programs. Surprisingly, I find the dictates of most diet regimens too daunting. I balk at being so focused on food—too much emphasis on buying it, preparing it, weighing it, and tracking it. The dieting dictates I have lived with all my life no longer seem to be stubbornly clinging to me.

Today, I hit the eighty-seventh day since I have purged. Technically, twelve weeks. I seemed to have moved away from the binge-purge cycle. And maybe the habit of mindful eating has taken a stronger hold than I had believed, as I seem to naturally gravitate to a more free-range style of eating. I eat what I want. I forgo the carrots if I crave a cookie. I slather peanut butter on toast and forgo the non-caloric butter spray if that's what I feel like eating.

And I wait to see if the brown skirt with the white polka dots continues to tighten.

Lingering Demons

Eddie lingers in the shadows, flirting with me to come back.

I go out to dinner with four of my girlfriends to celebrate two of their birthdays. It's been over three calendar months since I have purged. Tonight at dinner, I have a glass of wine and dessert.

The birthday girls pick two desserts: a generous slice of carrot cake, smothered in cream cheese frosting and one of those death-by-chocolate wonders oozing gooey caramel. We pass around each dessert. Though I don't take much onto my plate, my fork keeps stabbing at the carrot cake still left on the platter. (After all, if it's not actually on my plate, it doesn't really count.)

I leave with a protruding stomach and a slight case of dizziness as the sugar assaults my body. It is an unwelcome, yet strangely familiar, feeling. After all these months of carefully retraining my palate and monitoring my satiety level, random thoughts nevertheless whiz through my head as I pull into my driveway:

I could get rid of this so easily.

I could lie about it in my private therapy session.

When I go upstairs to greet my husband, I could pop a breath mint.

No one would ever know.

No one except for me.

I enter the front hall. I pass the half bath. I head toward the stairs. I remind myself how much physically stronger I feel. My jaw no longer cracks and aches. My shoulders and neck are regaining their mobility. My throat is no longer chronically hoarse.

"Goodnight, ED," I whisper, as I enter the bedroom.

And then I lean over and kiss the cheek of the only man in my life now—my husband.

The Shift Away From and To

The days turn into weeks; one-on-one therapy dwindles to once a month.

I think I have learned new adaptive strategies, but I am not sure.

I am more focused. I seem to be able to garner the strength to begin constructing the life I have always envisioned for myself. To check the things off my to-do list that have languished there too long.

I am able to circumvent past roadblocks and get out of my own way. I somehow find the time to streamline my computer files, take a fresh look at old and abandoned projects, toss meaningless mementos taking up valuable storage space in my home office.

I keep in mind perfection is not what I am seeking. But, I am allowing myself, encouraging myself, propelling myself to be the best I can be. I change my hair color, update my stodgy wardrobe, seek out advice on skin care and exfoliating.

I buy a bunch of flowers for my marble-topped credenza. I light heavily scented candles before I cook dinner. I impulsively purchase a marble and wood cutting board at an extravagant price—throwing out my scratched, plastic one—and marvel at the pleasure I now derive from chopping and slicing.

But the biggest surprise comes not from a shift in my purchasing habits—nor from living in a more sensory pleasing, better organized and more attractive environment—nor from displaying a more vibrant and bohemian demeanor. The inner change was reflected most strongly in the content of my monthly "Incidentally, Iris" columns I wrote during this transitional time. When I re-read them all one morning, I was stunned. Well over half of my columns had the same focus and underlying theme: engagement and re-engagement.

I was thrilled. I had internalized the mindfulness I had been exposed to. It was like finding my way when I didn't even know I had lost it.

Re-engaging to a Point

I watch my two-year-old granddaughter approach the world—with reckless and wild abandon and no regard for consequences. At Disney World, toddling through crowds, she heedlessly hurls herself among strangers, with little thought to parental proximity. Her two siblings, ages five and seven, willingly wander with the same sense of joyful wonder, but know the rules: stay within eyesight of a family member.

I am sixty-six years old. I, too, long to be as free-spirited as my two-year-old granddaughter, throwing myself into new and strange environments with wild and wily abandonment. Unlike her, I have been tainted by improper regard for consequences and planning. Unlike her, I have become comfortable with self-imposed boundaries. Maybe too much so, as I was soon to learn.

Checking my to-do list last Sunday evening, I realized I had an upcoming week free of doctors' appointments, bill paying, meetings and volunteer activities. Elated and relieved, I immediately scanned the local scene for ripe new experiences. I found two: a new type of yoga class and a mixed media art class. Registering online was a snap.

I rose early on Monday morning, savoring the giddy feeling of both learning something new and widening my social circle. As the morning progressed, however, strange new feelings emerged—apprehension, fear of the unfamiliar, and lack of confidence in my innate abilities to make it through. I regretted my impulsiveness and began questioning my ability to keep up with the rigors of the new level of yoga class I had committed to. And what in my right mind had ever prompted me to register for an art class I clearly was totally ill-equipped to tackle?

The funk lasted until Wednesday. Until I slid my yoga mat into the car. Until I gathered materials to tote to the collage class. And then my sense of gratitude for the privilege of retirement set in. And then my natural sense of "What the heck, I'll try it" attitude came roaring back.

In yoga, I clumsily executed the Downward Dog position, losing my balance more times than naught. And in art class, my ideas ran way ahead of my expertise, at times overwhelming me. But I made it through.

I basked in my success at stepping out of my self-imposed silo. And once home, I looked for a way to unwind. I spotted the unopened box in the corner of the family room—containing very old videos I had sent to a Tennessee company to get transferred to CDs. But because so many beloved family members had passed away since those happy times, I was reluctant to tackle the viewing of Thanksgiving gatherings and my parent's fiftieth wedding anniversary party. And because my sons were now scattered all over the country—not just steps away from my bedroom door—I knew watching them take their first steps, foray into little league baseball and recite their Bar Mitzvah Torah portion would engender an intense longing to be back in the child-rearing fray.

Should I venture on?

Turning back the clock is not possible. Pining for the past is not healthy. My two-year-old granddaughter doesn't get that, nor in all probability do her siblings. But I am in the seventh decade of my life and that's one consequence I understand only too well. So I settle instead for watching season two of *Orange Is the New Black*. There is no chance of me longing to be embroiled in the throes of emotional entanglements and in the confinement of a physical prison.

It seems the safest choice for now.

Re-engaging With Our Dog

When our fourth son, Sam—who boomeranged back home—unexpectedly brought home a Labrador Retriever puppy, I was less than overjoyed. He assured me she was house-trained; I then watched in horror as she took a major dump on the family room sisal rug. I was furious. That was three years ago and she's still with us, though not much has changed.

In the early weeks, we observed Lola's behavior. She loyally followed Sam around everywhere in the house. She cried shamelessly when he left her and yelped joyously when he returned. When he gave her the least little bit of attention, she responded with wild enthusiasm. When he wasn't around, she morosely lumbered back to his room, snuggling under a pile of his dirty clothes or slinking back into her oversized cage. I kept harping on the fact that her behavior was inappropriate and bordering on offensive and sarcastically suggested Sam put her on an anti-depressant. Sam sullenly refused, unfazed by my outburst. As was Lola.

"Big mistake," I shouted at him.

When Sam inquired about her behavior when at doggie day care, Sam was assured by the caretakers that Lola consistently was a model of friendliness to all the other dogs and regularly exhibited leadership ability, unbridled exuberance and social engagement. I found that hard to believe. We got indifference. And we got ignored. There was so little interaction that my husband and I began not-so-jokingly to refer to her as "the non-dog." That was three years ago and she is still with us, though not much has changed.

My husband tried many tactics. And he diligently incorporated into his behavior all the suggestions the vet offered on establishing a firmer bond with Lola—being the one to feed her, going with her on long, solitary walks, playing catch in the side yard, taking her and picking her up at doggie day care. He even went as far as habitually going into Sam's room each morning and night to lie beside her, talking softly. He was consistent in his routine dealings with her. He approached cautiously. He initiated no sudden movements. He spoke quietly.

On the other hand, I mostly ignored her and she ignored me. I didn't talk to a vet, read pet-owning manuals, search the Internet for answers. Still, I was bothered by her idiosyncratic ways. If I had friends over, she indifferently glanced at them and then meandered away. It was embarrassing. If I gave her a bone to chew on, she took it and sailed past me with nary a backward glance. It was disappointing. If I answered her scratches to be let in after being on the porch, she slunk past me as she made a bee line for Sam's room. It was disheartening.

If I longed for anything more, I was unaware of it until I began listening to other pet owner's stories of affectionate bonding and joyous interaction. Barking loudly and protectively in their defense. Laying at their feet on a cold winter night. Hovering close by at dinner. It was painful to acknowledge how little we were getting back from Lola. That was three years ago and she is still with us, though not much has changed.

The other day, Sam had just left for work and I walked to the front door on my way to watering the plants. Surprisingly, Lola had not immediately retreated to Sam's room at the sound of the garage door closing. She was waiting patiently at the door for Sam's return—though it would be many hours. When she saw me approach, she rolled over, put her hind legs up in the air and gently placed her front paw on my arm. Instinctively, but tentatively, I began to stroke her underbelly. She relaxed further into the floor and her body went at ease. We continued in this manner for minutes. Me stroking. Her breathing rhythmically. And then I roused myself to go water the plants and she galloped up the front stairs to Sam's room.

What did I learn from this encounter? Interacting with your dog is like interacting with your adult kids. Lower your expectations. Stop comparing. Accept their quirks. Embrace their essence. Savor the interactions. Be ready to engage when the opportunity is offered. And let the rest go.

Re-engaging With My Husband "Ain't" So Easy

My dad will be ninety in October. He is getting weaker and more detached. I notice he is less interested in the nightly news, more prone to infection, and increasingly depressed over his lack of energy. This journal entry isn't about him, however, at least not directly. It's more about coming to terms with what my life will look like in the aftermath of losing him. It's about recognizing that sometime soon there will be one less person in this world that loves me unconditionally.

How will I fill that gap?

One way, I surmise, is to cherish what I have and hold it close. My thoughts turn to my husband—a pretty likely person for me to look to in my soul searching. I know I was a devoted daughter. Am I a devoted wife? I think about all the things I do that maybe an "ideal" wife would scoff at, shudder and shun.

Most nights when my husband is at home, I'm either at a work function, out with my female friends, or holed up in the living room with an enthralling new book. Or I'm busy binge-watching all the TV shows I've recorded. And I get mighty grumpy at any conversational interruptions.

Or I'm furiously organizing yet another closet, or scrutinizing my ever-growing to-do list, or concocting innovative ways to maintain a modicum of closeness with my precious grandchildren, who live 900 miles away.

My husband and I rarely eat dinner together and during the day if we do communicate, it's by short, terse emails or texts. We, too, are victims of instant gratification and short attention spans.

Okay. So we spend every Saturday together without fail—it's our day to play, indulge, do whatever we want. Explicitly, not to tackle one single, solitary item on our chore list, unless we both mutually agree we want to.

Okay. In our defense, we just instituted date night. Every Wednesday, we meet for dinner at a new place. Our only rule is that we can't talk about any family members. All other topics are fair game. It is remarkable the plethora of subjects we can cover in depth in an hour when I am deprived of complaining about relatives.

So maybe my marriage isn't as pathetic as I originally surmised. At least that was my conclusion after skimming through my latest, most favorite self-help book: *The Secret Lives of Wives*, by Iris Krasnow. The subtitle is *Women Share What it Takes to Really Stay Married*.

It's a compelling topic, especially when Krasnow reminds us that, with our increasing longevity, most of us will be married longer that most people used to live. And it's a sobering subject: how to not only live "happily ever after" amidst the inevitable bumps and roadblocks, but, in addition, keeping your vows "without killing someone first!"

If you have guts and are capable of surviving the exhausting tedium of child-rearing, you too can sail through marital storms and reach a safe harbor. Here's some essential cargo to bring along, according to Krasnow:

- A strong sense of an evolving self, apart from the marital relationship
- A willingness to embrace adventures in uncharted territory
- Friendships with both sexes
- Work you are passionate about
- A dedication to learning new skills
- Keen and tested navigational skills

It's a lot easier to appreciate each other when the homework wars have ceased, there are no nightly bottle feedings or disruptive calls from errant teenagers. It's a lot easier, once you have years of shared history together, to recognize that in spite of the annoyances, irritations and petty squabbles, you cherish the history you and your partner have built together. The map exists. You know the obstacles to avoid. The boundaries not to cross. You know the waves won't topple you, even if you get submerged for a moment or two. You know where the lighthouses are to guide you safely home and where the undertows are to be avoided.

Barbara Bush once said a formula for longevity was picking the right partner in the first place. The second time around, I did.

Krasnow points out that the happiest period in marriage comes when you stick it out. But, she reiterates, in spite of finding that soul mate, a good marriage takes constant work. Like one of Krasnow's funniest friends says, "Marriage is like a hot bath. Once you get into it and get used to it, it's not so hot anymore."

However, no matter what the temperature of the water, I've never found anything to come remotely close to the pleasure of a soaking bath—except, of course, my long, chaotic, duke-it-out-at-all-costs marriage.

Too bad I felt I couldn't bring my husband alongside me as I battled my bulimia. My fear of losing him overrode the pull of letting him in.

To Cut or Not to Cut?

Just a few weeks into private counseling, I start thinking about cutting the therapeutic tie altogether.

Five Months

It's been five months since I have binged and purged.

Craving for sweets still lingers. And when I give in to the craving, I still eat furtively and too fast.

I recently babysat for two of my grandchildren. Their kitchen is a well-spring of tempting goodies. Having just celebrated my granddaughter's second birthday, the granite counter sported a half-eaten birthday cake overloaded with gooey vanilla icing—one of a myriad of foods that easily weaken my resolve.

The kids were bathed, smothered with kisses and put to bed. All was quiet. I circled the kitchen counter—trying to ward off the desire to plow into the rich, layered cake.

I gave in, eating mindlessly and quickly, hardly giving myself time to luxuriate in the absolute ecstasy of the cake's richness.

Keeping it down was a commitment I had made to myself and I did not waver.

Who knows, maybe next time I decide to overindulge I can surrender to the moment and do it with great fanfare and pleasure.

Six Months

I am eating what I want, but with some restraint.

I still can't tolerate being intensely hungry. So, like someone prescribed pain pills, I stay in front of it. I eat before I am consumed with hunger pangs.

I very seldom find myself ravenously hungry. When I do, I ask myself what needs filling up and why. It's usually centered on lack of communication with my grown children. So I pick up the phone and call, or increase my text messages to them, or engage them in an email exchange.

I am beginning to think intuitive eating can be a permanent way of life, no longer an unattainable, unsustainable goal.

A Chink Appears

My dad's sick.

I cancel plans for the sixty-fifth birthday I had planned for myself, take a leave of absence from my job and fly back to Ohio to help my mother care for my dad.

I watch this once energetic, articulate man flail helplessly in physical therapy. I watch him unsuccessfully battle a urinary infection that spreads mercilessly. I watch my mother watching him as an aide probes, prods, bathes, dresses and feeds this once fiercely independent character. (And I do mean character.)

We confer with doctors, seek second opinions, scour the Internet for answers. To no avail.

My dad perks up momentarily when all my sons come to town to visit him for a long weekend, regaling him with tales of their business dealings. When they depart, however, his spirits sag. Every day after that he is weaker, more detached, and more despairing.

My sister and I do not see eye-to-eye on my dad's care. We exchange heated barbs that quickly turn combative and adversarial. I am shocked; my sister is the one person in my life I have never fought with. What is happening?

ED beckons alluringly. I turn away from him reluctantly, forcing myself to engage my sister in further conversation.

She and I uneasily try to achieve a compromise, to resolve our differences in relating to my dad's care. It is not easy. We have no roadmap for discussing disagreements. We have always just deflected any grievances, waiting for time to take the edge off our anger. This time we don't have that luxury. We sit face-to-face. We go through each point of contention. We prioritize what needs to be decided. We each express our opinion. We listen. And then decide together on our next course of action. We make up amidst tears and hugs.

As I head back to my dad's room, I run into ED in the hall. I push past him brusquely. I am trading the veneer of perfection for the durability of a real relationship—a relationship that can withstand bumps and bruises without falling apart. I don't need ED's one-sided devotion. I am learning that perfect relationships are not real relationships.

Early in the fall, my dad slips into a coma and is brought to a hospice facility. My mother continues her daily trek to see him, wearing a face bright with carefully applied makeup so, if my father does manage a peek, he will see her as "bearing up." It is a facade that she keeps up faithfully, while murmuring to him that he will be fine.

Twenty-one days later, he is still lingering in a coma.

A minister visits the hospice center. Though we are Jewish, he sits down with us. He listens to our concerns and our desire to in some way hasten the end.

He asks a question: "Is there anyone he has not said goodbye to?"

We pause and think.

"Perhaps," I reply, "my uncle, my dad's youngest brother. He has not been able to travel due to his own health constraints. And my husband, who has not been back to see him in a couple of weeks."

"Call both of them," he suggests, "and ask them to call him and tell him goodbye. It may be what he is waiting for. And it may hasten the process."

That same afternoon, we call my uncle and put the phone up to my dad's ear. The whole conversation lasts only about thirty seconds, but we notice a light fluttering of my father's eyelids.

Next, we call my husband and explain the situation. He complies, but the anguish in his voice is apparent. Their conversation seems to go on for hours, though afterwards I realize it has only been mere minutes. My father is unresponsive and I hear my husband doing all the talking. He recalls the many moments they shared in business, the lunches spent strategizing, the disagreements they had that years later they laughed about. I hear him thanking my dad for teaching him the real estate appraisal business and so readily welcoming him into our family.

"I love you, Pike," he sobbingly concludes. I gently remove the phone from my dad's ear as I notice one lone tear sliding down his cheek.

My dad passed away peacefully that evening—a half hour after my mom and sister and I left to grab some dinner. Minutes after his caregiver stepped out of room to take a short break.

Overnight, our family loses the patriarch. My sons lose a cherished role model. My grandchildren lose a great-grandfather they will remember best through the video my cousin made documenting my dad's experience in World War II as a ball turret gunner on a B-17. My siblings and I lose an anchor and my mother loses the man she married when she was seventeen.

ED sees an opening in my armor.

The Art of Coping

My dad taught me the art of coping. How ironic that he, also a master at coping, used food for solace.

Neither my brother nor sister had a fascination with food, though my brother had a close relationship with the liquor bottle which waxed and waned over the years. My sister was a skinny kid and a picky eater, until she met her husband and he introduced her to a wide range of different foods.

My mom was comfortable with food. She ate when hungry, stopped when full, practiced moderation in portions naturally and had a life-long image of herself as slim and trim, even when she was not. This was diametrically opposed to my mindset. I had a lifelong image of myself as big and fat even at times when I wasn't. I was uncomfortable around food. I ate with no regard to my physical hunger. And I never stopped eating until the plate was wiped clean.

My dad's weight was like a yo-yo—up and down. He was the first one to sit down for dinner, the fastest eater of the five of us and, when at a restaurant, always the first one at the buffet table. Maybe it was his upbringing during the Great Depression that fueled his compulsive need to eat or maybe, like me, he equated food with comfort and security. I will never know. He's dead now and I never thought to ask him.

As far as I know, he never purged, but he regularly left the dinner table admonishing himself that he had once again eaten too much.

Ironically, what worked for him would end up working for me. My mom recently confided in me that he was one of the first men to join the local chapter of Weight Watchers in the 1960s and successfully lost over thirty pounds. He was not a joiner by nature—nor am I. How interesting that we both swept past our natural inclination to shun the group experience, embraced Weight Watchers and succeeded in shedding pounds.

No matter what the needle on the scale registered, I always felt conflicted. ED was my constant companion—the enabling force that allowed me to "keep coping." And though I appeared confident, highly functioning and relaxed, I was not on the inside what I appeared to be on the outside.

I wonder if my dad had an "ED" in his life and whether he felt the same way.

September 2012

Not surprisingly, I think about my dad a lot in the days following his funeral.

One of my earliest memories is of my father telling me something.

"You're run-of-the-mill, Iris," he would say. "Just run-of-the-mill."

Maybe this was my first lesson in intuition, insight and savvy. I knew by the way he said it that what he actually meant was, "You're special. Very special."

And he knew I knew. And so the dance began.

In 1947, my father was a young GI coming home from Europe to his war bride, my mother. I was born within a year of his returning stateside—part of the first wave of baby boomers.

Eventually my mom and dad moved out of my grandparent's house into their own place. The wooden kitchen cabinets were painted yellow. A lazy susan was bought for Sunday night dinners of corned beef, pickles and rye bread. A deep maroon paisley couch with tassels was picked out and delivered.

So was a metal swing set. Unassembled.

The metal swing set is new, bright, shiny, massive, and all mine.

My dad works all day assembling the metal monster as I sit and watch. After hours of tedious labor, he digs four holes in which to place the swing set's main poles. To my surprise, he sets the poles in concrete.

Most dads just dug a shallow hole and set the swing set's main support poles in the dirt. The higher the swing went, the more the poles wiggled, vibrated and lifted out of the hole. Swinging kids squeaked with terror and delight as the whole structure rose, shuttered and fell back into place. I was always afraid that one day one of those entire swing sets would just tumble over.

Perhaps sensing my fear, my dad grounds my swing set in concrete so I can swing as high as I want, unencumbered by fear of the entire mass becoming airborne.

I plant my bottom on the red metal seat. The heat from the metal stings the backs of my bare legs. I grimace. I squirm a little from side to side. The toes of my clean white Keds brush the grass. I bend my knees and swing my feet forward. Lean back and push off. I start the climb to the sky—head tilted back to see the great blue expanse—my ponytail waving wildly from side to side.

"Okay, Daddy. You can push me now," I scream. "Real high. I'm ready."

The years pass. The grass underneath the swing set is matted down. Then worn away. Then reduced to finely-ground brown grains that look like home plate on a kid's makeshift baseball field. The red seats are not as shiny. The supporting poles have a few dents from my swinging crazy. And rust spots are starting to appear.

I still swing.

The years pass. I graduate. Go to college. Marry. Divorce. Remarry. I have the kids and bake the cookies. And do the wash. And drive the car pools.

Always with back-up, behind-the-scenes coaching from my dad:

- Never let them see you sweat
- Make it look easy
- Do it your way
- Do it

Years pass. The kids move away. I still come home to visit.

The swing set is now old and rickety. The push-off mound is sunken in with shallow gullies. The chains are disjointed. The rust is heavy. The seats hang crooked.

The swing set, like me, is well past the half century mark. We are both defined, grounded, centered and structured. Marked by age. Touched by exposure to the elements. Lopsided. A little rickety. Still functional.

I walk into the backyard unnoticed. I spot the metal monster, which now seems so diminished in size. I approach the red seat warily. It looks so small. Can it hold me? I settle in. Squirm around. Slowly push off and up. I arch my back and hang on tight.

"Okay Daddy," I say softly to myself. "You can push me now. Real high. I'm ready."

My father gave me a firm foundation on which to grow. And wings with which to soar. Without him, I would never have had the motivation, the zest, and the inspiration to get through life. Much less enjoy it.

I am honoring my dad's memory by reinforcing my resolve to keep ED at bay.

Tripping the Scales Not Fantastic

I weigh 150 pounds. This is the most I have ever weighed other than when I was pregnant.

Blip

Lime green cargo pants and nine months to the day I stopped purging.

There is a connection between the two.

The pants are my fat pants and right now I am at my highest non-pregnancy weight ever. My lime green cargo pants are the only pair of pants I own that comfortably fit. Nine months to the day I stopped purging, I came the closest to doing it again. I went to a three-course tasting and ate everything in sight, and then came home and ate more. I was so stressed from my self-induced food-binge coma that I fell into bed without taking off my makeup and without brushing my teeth.

Where did this bout of self-destruction come from?

I have spent months re-acquainting myself with food. Finding out what I like. Trying not to live in a state of food deprivation. Not weighing myself.

And what's the outcome of all these good intentions???? Gaining an additional ten pounds piled onto the ten I gained during treatment.

Fucking great.

Clearly, I do not have as much control over what I put into my mouth as I would like. But I am not abandoning my original plan: I will not purge. Under any circumstances.

And maybe, just maybe, I will exercise more.

Pointer Panic

One hundred fifty-two pounds.

Without shoes.

Without my watch.

On an empty stomach.

All I wanted to do was snuggle under the covers and cry. I forced myself out of my familiar bed and out of my despairing head.

Methodically, I reviewed my options.

The diet doc down the street who gave out B12 shots and put his patients on a strict diet regimen, excluding coffee and gum. Nope.

The local pharmacy, which carried over-the-counter fat-burning appetite suppressants. Nope.

The neighborhood gym just a few blocks from my house, holding early morning boot camps. Nope.

The plastic surgeon who sucks fat out of your tummy. Nope.

I had just spent the last nine months dipping my toes back into real life and where did it get me?

I had just spent the last nine months re-acquainting myself with foods, and the joy of eating and tasting and savoring. I didn't eat badly. If I went out to lunch, instead of ordering a salad with a scoop of tuna and going light on the dressing, I broke out—sampling a grilled vegetable panini sandwich and savoring the oil semi-drenching it.

Guzzling down a malt every once in a while. Throwing a handful of licorice in my mouth before bedtime. Indulging in a few small bags of chips as I watched the evening news.

I had just spent the last nine months training myself to look forward to meals out, instead of dreading them. To participate in social occasions, even though I knew tempting goodies assailed my senses.

Where did it get me? It got me in a state of shock when I finally scooped up the courage to plant both feet on the scale. And look down.

It was beginning to make sense. Along with all my experimental revamping, I had to admit I had also just spent the last nine months gradually growing out of almost all the clothes in my closet. And the other half that used to hang loosely were now snug. Even my husband, who thinks my obsession with weight is a very boring subject, had noticed the weight gain. Still I had put off weighing myself.

So now I was getting desperate. Putting off reduced portions and increased exercise were no longer palatable. Delaying tackling the challenge of how to achieve what I had so longed to be—thin—was no longer an option.

If I had overcome the binge-purge cycle, I could triumph in this too.

Soon I would find a way. Soon I would realize I had indeed come a lot further than I had thought.

It all started the very next day.

The Day Before the Very Next Day

I wake up early.

I roll out of bed.

The aching joint pain in my knees reminds me of my increased girth.

I groan.

I pour myself a cup of coffee and review the last year.

I have been binge/purge free for almost one year.

What worked?

Accountability and acceptance.

That same formula should work for this most pressing challenge: losing weight. Getting back to a weight I feel comfortable with. Because in my heart, I know the truth. If I can't do this, I will succumb to ED's charms yet again.

Accountability and acceptance.

I don't need Alcoholics Anonymous. I am not a drinker.

What's the counterpart when weight is the issue?

I began to search for the answer.

The Very Next Day

While I am searching for answers, I start a new regimen. It seemed reasonable, consisting of eating smaller portions five times a day, drinking eight glasses of water daily, and for exercise either walking or yoga. Going light on the carbohydrates, heavy on raw veggies and staying away from all desserts was also part of my strategic plan.

I had given myself the gift of freedom from ED. Now I was determined to give myself the gift of looking the best I could, while being mindful of my health.

I was excited about my new endeavor. I loaded the freezer with bags of veggies. I threw out all the leftover Halloween candy. I banished every cookie and cracker in sight. And I bought a new, colorful pair of walking shoes and a to-die-for yoga pullover that complemented my new yoga mat. And sometimes, I even exceeded eight glasses of water a day.

I was on a roll. Imbued with determination, I sallied forth, wholeheartedly embracing my new lifestyle. There was only one problem: it didn't work. My brown skirt with the white polka dots remained stubbornly tight and unyielding.

I soon realized I had to pull the shade down on my newfound lifestyle. Self-monitoring was not working. I had to focus on re-creating what had worked in therapy: outside acceptance and accountability. And I had to find a way to lose weight and to keep it off.

If I didn't or couldn't, I knew that parting ways with ED would only be a temporary interlude in a life with a devil-like lover.

Weight Watchers "Points" the "Weigh"

After treatment, I had continued to experiment by eating what I wanted when I wanted. And to my delight, my hunger pains arrived at regular intervals—kinda like labor pains.

- 10 a.m.
- 1 p.m.
- 5 p.m.
- 7 p.m.
- 11 p.m.

Give or take a few minutes, these were my peak hunger times. I got so adept at picking up the beginnings of my stomach rumblings that I contemplated abandoning my watch. Other things accompanied the hunger pains—loss of concentration for the task at hand and a low threshold of frustration. And I observed that if I ate enough I could feel full and easily make it until the next deadline.

This pattern worked well to satisfy my sense of progress with the bulimic-free lifestyle I was striving for. Unfortunately, it wreaked havoc on my waistline and hips. Every couple of weeks I eliminated more clothes from my wardrobe—zippers refused to stay zipped. Buttons wouldn't close. Blouses pulled tightly across my bust. But it was the avocado green capri pants that finally forced me to face how fat I had gotten—the ones that literally fell off my hips when I began outpatient treatment and now were snug against my girth.

Panic ensued.

I reverted back to my default mechanism when needing a barometer of my self-worth—the scale. I stripped down to my birthday suit. I didn't dare drink my morning eight ounces of water accompanied by my antacid pill. I unstrapped my watch. Unhooked my earrings. Slipped off my rings. And stepped on the scale.

I was horrified.

Tears streaming down my face, yelling at the top of my lungs, beating every pillow on my bed with violent thrusts only sapped my energy but not my despair. I was desperate. All I wanted to do was plop down on the couch with a gallon of ice cream wedged beside me and start scooping the cold, smooth, soothing contents right down my throat.

The realization hit me hard: The only way I could permanently banish ED was to be able to control my appetite and maintain a pleasing weight. And north of 150 pounds on a five-foot, one-inch frame wasn't it.

At this juncture, I had been binge- and purge-free for almost one year. I would like to say I utilized the numeric proof of my ability to succeed to spur me on to reach a reasonable weight loss goal. But the horror of the scale overrode any victories I had attained in fighting my obsession.

I fell into a state of miserable and unrelenting despair. I stopped calling friends. I snapped at my husband continuously. I read the newspaper and was only comforted by the bad news—of recession, murder, bankruptcy and terroristic mayhem. I avoided the comics, lifestyle features and any article that even smacked of self-improvement.

I didn't binge. And I didn't purge.

But once again, my relationship with the scale had sabotaged my achievements. Nothing mattered but that I was fat. Ordinary to look at. Easily passed over. Nothing special. And my insides resonated with what my outside had become. I labored over word flow while writing my monthly slice-of-life column. Skeins of multi-colored yarn remained packed away in bags, far from the knitting needles they were meant to embrace. My houseplants withered from desultory watering.

Weeks passed. I wallowed. I shrugged off suggestions for moving forward. I cried. I thrashed. I raged. I exuded toxicity.

Waking up one morning toward the end of December, I waited for the knot in my stomach to appear and my thoughts to go virally negative. To my total surprise, my insides weren't fluttering with unease that morning. My limbs felt ready to dance, not drag. And an unfamiliar just-do-it spirit coursed through my veins.

"I can find a way through this hell," I chanted to myself. "I can find a way."

And I did.

In January 2013, I attended a Weight Watchers meeting for the first time. I may not have been the most hopeful one at that meeting, but I certainly would bet I was one of the most determined. I had not come this far in beating a forty-six-year-long eating disorder to remain heavier than I wanted to be.

I learned my target weight is based on my height, my current weight, my age and gender. Considering those variables, I wanted to set a goal of getting down to 130 pounds. But the good people at Weight Watchers are savvy. "Just set the goal to lose five percent of your current weight initially," my instructor suggested. "Although your ultimate goal may be more, going in five percent increments is less daunting."

That was the easy part.

Realizing it would probably take me until the fall to get to my goal was the hard part. How long could I keep this diet going?

That was my first misconception. Weight Watchers shuns the term diet. Eating to lose weight is a goal. Maintaining that weight is a way of life.

Weight Watchers provides acceptance, structure and the accountability I needed. And it perfectly fit my needs. I was looking for a way to measure what I ate. I was looking for a way to calculate how much I could take in without gaining weight. I was looking for a way to eat less but feel full so I could ultimately shrink the girth. Weight Watchers provided the can-do tools.

I wholeheartedly embraced the idea that Weight Watchers espoused: weight loss is just one part of long-term weight management. Weight Watchers embraces the philosophy of a healthy lifestyle—mentally, emotionally and physically. I was right "on board" with that. Clean slate looking for chalk. And they provided the chalk.

I needed to start instituting some habitual actions—a routine—that would help me gain some perspective on portion control and some quantitative idea of what I could eat each day to begin to lose weight at a steady but not necessarily rapid pace. At the beginning, I couldn't trust my own brain to tell me when I was full. I surmised that's how I landed at hovering around 150 pounds in the first place.

Weight Watchers emphasizes tracking what you eat. Writing down every morsel that enters your mouth. The concept is simple: write down what you eat because studies have shown that people who write down what they eat, eat less. Everything you pick up and pop into your mouth counts. Knowing that, you are much less apt to grab a mini-donut, break off a piece of chocolate, grab the last remaining uneaten piece of steak on your spouse's plate.

Every food has a numeric point attached to it, except most fruits and vegetables. To lose weight, Weight Watchers helps you calculate your magic number—the maximum number of points you can take in each day and still lose weight. Mine was eighteen. Tracking what I ate forced me to pay attention to my hunger and the accumulation of points. When I finished a meal or snack, I saw what I had eaten. I noted when I was still hungry and when I was full. And acted accordingly.

The greatest gift: Weight Watchers gives you bonus points each day. You can save them throughout the week to splurge on one big delight or use them each day if you are still hungry. I never once accumulated them. I applied them daily for my eleven p.m. snacks—a lifesaver for me. I had something to look forward to all day and I never once went to bed with gnawing pangs of hunger.

Environments impact me. I spend countless waking hours poring over home decorating magazines, arranging or re-arranging knick-knacks, chairs and pictures. I explore creative ways to enhance my home's ambiance and functionality. So Weight Watchers' initiative of setting up your surroundings for success appealed to me intellectually and artistically.

Here are a few tips I adopted immediately.

I removed tempting food from clear sight. The M&Ms in the glass canister were replaced with hard candy—cheap ones that scratched the top of your mouth when you sucked them—but still provided a pleasing punch of color in my kitchen. Foods I could eat in unlimited amounts were placed eye level on my most conveniently accessible refrigerator shelf and displayed attractively. Pears and apples got a cut glass bowl and the strawberries were washed and housed in a funky ceramic container I picked up at an art fair. All were ready to be plucked and eaten in one fell swoop.

Hard boiled eggs were artfully stacked in an off-white basket to match their shells. Cheese, peanut butter crackers and cookies were hidden away, along with my husband's ice cream and caramels. Bananas on the verge of becoming overripe were cut up and frozen to use in my Weight Watcher shakes—a treat I indulged in one to two times daily.

I embraced the idea of weight loss-friendly actions becoming part of my daily routine. I labeled food I cooked or used often with the point counts until I had memorized them and then went on to the next batch of food items. I planned ahead when I was eating out. I made sure to never attend a dinner party hungry. And when I was really vigilant, I ate without reading something or watching TV. Just savoring the taste of the food. I tried to eat by taking a sip of water between each bite—but that was way too annoying. But I did manage to introduce one major eating habit into my routine: I did not put anything else in my mouth until I had swallowed what I had originally put in my mouth—my sister told me that one.

And most importantly, I put my faith in the professionals at Weight Watchers, who were living proof that behavior can be changed and weight lost and maintained. I was thrilled to see that you were encouraged NOT to starve but to use your minimum amount of points every day. My fear of hunger was diminished just knowing that there were some things I could eat with no point value at all—ideal for when hunger wasn't the reason I was stuffing down excess food.

There were certain foods I had grown attached to over the course of my outpatient bulimia treatment. Foods I was not willing to give up because they satisfied me greatly: pineapple-flavored Greek yogurt and hazelnut Coffeemate in my coffee. Not the fat-free kind. Not the sugar-free kind. To my delight, I didn't have to. I just made sure I counted their accrued points.

So this was my plan: Just do it. Don't own the outcome. Honor the journey. Stick with the regimen. I had no idea how easily it would come off nor how much I would struggle with the confinements of the points, but I allowed myself to be patient and hopeful. Buoyed by the other struggling dieters in my class and the instructor's guidance, I watched with glee as the pounds began to shed.

Quickly? Not quickly enough.

But steadily—a half pound here. Every once in a while a two-pound loss. A quarter-pound loss. And so it went. Almost every week I lost something—even if it was only an ounce or two.

By fall, I had reached my goal of weighing in at 130 pounds. By now, tracking the foods I was eating and the point count was a habit.

Do I still track my points and write down what I eat? Most of the time. And the times I sloppily tracked my points, partially listed what I ate, eyeballed the portion size instead of weighed it, didn't count the nibbles of Oreos and mouse bites of Snickers bar—well, the scale crept north once again. I reinstated Weight Watchers suggestions and guidelines, and the brown skirt with the white polka dots loosened up.

I try and drink six glasses of water a day. I still have my diet orange soda each night after dinner. I chew too much sugarless gum, usually two to three sticks at a time. I still use way too much salt. And every once in a while, I binge on my husband's caramels even though they are tucked away in the pantry. Or I eat two pieces of the leftover home-made chocolate cake I froze in the freezer in the garage, hoping I would forget about it.

Do I still feel much better on the inside when I look thinner on the outside? Yes.

Do I still have an obsession with the scale? Yes. Going to a Weight Watchers physical location to weigh in monthly is still a great source of angst. I go first thing in the morning. I forgo my morning cup of coffee to cut any excess ounces. And I always wear my brown skirt with the white polka dots. I try to prepare myself for the outcome by checking the prominence of my cheekbones in the mirror before departing. And I always take off my watch before weighing in at my neighborhood Weight Watchers location. I fight through the nervous stomach flutters and the fear engulfing me when I step on the digital scale. Watching as the numbers configure themselves into my final weight remains an agonizing ordeal.

Some old habits die hard. Thank goodness, they are not the deadly ones.

365 Days Without ED

February 14, 2013.

This day marks the one-year anniversary of my breakup with ED.

For many weeks I had pondered how to mark the day. I thought about writing a letter to each of my sons detailing my struggles. I vacillated about sharing my ultimate decision to seek treatment. I longed to share the glory with them of being out from under the clutches of ED.

Something holds me back.

What if our breakup is temporary and ED lures me back in?

What purpose is there to telling them? Who knows? It could alienate rather than unite them with me.

I'm passing on this course of action. For now.

What do I do to mark the day?

I decide to reward myself by buying a piece of jewelry. I decide that for every day I have not binged and purged I would spend a dollar. Three hundred and sixty-five dollars. Surely, I reason, what I saved in food costs since ceasing to binge and purge will more than cover the cost of my indulgence.

A boutique in the mall, specializing in jewelry from Spain, grabs my attention. Thirty minutes later, I emerge with a funky necklace—ropes of colorful leather entwined with silver, encrusted with beads.

I wear it for six straight days and then I find a very visible location in my jewelry box to put it so I can easily access it.

The Weigh Is the Way

The last time I was happy with my weight was August 5, 1947, at approximately eight-thirteen in the morning—the moment I was born. Long and lanky, I weighed in at five pounds, fifteen ounces.

Too bad I was unaware of the lifelong deleterious effect the scale would have on me. If I had that awareness, I probably would not have been howling upon emerging from the womb, but beaming from ear to ear.

My skinny stage was short-lived. By the age of seven, my body was beginning to blossom, and beginning to betray me. Though I was one of the fastest runners in my grade, I was plumping up and shooting up. My fifty-yard dash record would soon be broken by a leaner classmate. And my fragile image of myself as average size would soon be shattered too. It happened one Sunday morning when my dad took me with him on one of his deals. He was selling a couple's small business for them and needed some papers signed. Politely, the husband asked how

I liked middle school. A deadly, awkward silence ensued. "Nah," my dad uneasily quipped, "she's not there yet. We just grow 'em big in the country." Mortified, I fled to the car. I was in second grade.

It's easy for rich people to say money isn't everything. And, it's easy for naturally thin people to discount the effect of the scale's upward climb on a weight-battling person's mood, temperament, social life and lifestyle. It didn't take me long to realize big girls and fat girls didn't garner the kind of attention I was seeking. But it wasn't until years later that I fully comprehended the power of the pound. Or should I say the power of the excess pound.

Take my friend Kathy. She had been heavy most of her life. Having a lean and fit husband who liked to party, she dutifully accompanied him on his forays. Most of the time, she confided to me, people gave her a friendly hello and then kinda ignored her for the rest of the evening.

Kathy is intelligent, witty and well-read. An objective bystander would readily describe her as an interesting conversationalist. All these positive attributes went unnoticed until Kathy lost thirty-five pounds. Then, suddenly, the people she had been socializing with for years were captivated by her vignettes, her opinions, her point of view.

The character Tevye in *Fiddler on the Roof*, exclaims, "Just because you're rich, they think you know." Ditto for weight. Just because you're thin, they think you know, too. A person of normal weight confers an aura of being in control, well-adjusted, intact, functional and conversation-worthy. At best, an overweight person is often met with indifference and lack of acknowledgment. At worst, with derision, ridicule and contempt.

I was weight-obsessed. The trusty old bathroom scale was the barometer of my mood. It clouded my vision. Distorted my self-image. When it registered north, it, depressed my spirits. When it registered south of my ideal, I worried hysterically how to maintain it. So I starved. Felt deprived. Binged. Vomited. Stepped on the scale. Over and over again.

I am not sure why, but sometime in my thirties, I threw out the scale and stopped weighing myself. I think I was tired of the scale's minute fluctuations so dramatically altering my mood. But the scale had always been the measuring stick as to how good or bad I felt about myself. What would be my measuring stick now?

I'd like to say I weaned myself away from relating my self-worth to my weight, but at that point I was only capable of changing the yardstick to a less precise one: the depth of my cheekbones and the fit of my brown skirt with the white polka dots. As long as my cheekbones remained prominent when gazing in the mirror, and as long as I could still easily zip up and button my brown skirt with the white polka dots, I was in the acceptable zone.

For a while, I even put off annual visits to my gynecologist for fear of getting weighed, but inventiveness rescued me. I figured out I could get on the scale, close my eyes, and not see where the needle stopped. And I always made sure to request in advance from the nurse that she not disclose my weight to me, though I gave her permission to cite it in my chart.

I was beginning to find my "way."

The Perils of Retirement

Shortly after my dad's death, I shakily return to my job—a step that's difficult after my three-month leave of absence over the summer. In my position, summer months are planning months; the fall, a time for implementing. I resume work with the same responsibilities I always had, but no backup plans to rely on. I begin sleeping fitfully, worried that I am disappointing my colleagues and that my work product smacks of inefficiency.

"What," I wonder, "would my father advise me to do in this situation?"

My father taught me how critical it is to think clearly, unemotionally and logically when faced with a difficult issue. It worked. When I was contemplating divorcing my first husband, my father was the one who reminded me that "It was a cold, cruel world out there." And he emphasized that long after I took the advice of friends and family members to break up my marriage, all those same friends and family members would still have their husbands to go home to. I'd no longer have mine.

When I made the final break with my first husband, my father's realistic perspective prepared me for the confusion, loneliness and sadness a newly-divorced person inevitably experiences.

Following my dad's template for dealing with rising job pressure, I consider retirement. Cost-of-living calculations reveal I can swing early retirement. I give considerable thought to what my retirement will actually look like. Quite simply: unstructured time. Lots of it. It's been fifteen months since I have binged and purged. Am I ready to be rudderless? With no set routine? Will ED come courting?

I remember my father's admonition to slow down when making changes—take sustained mouse steps to reach my goal, not kangaroo leaps. So, first, I ponder what I think my retirement will actually look like.

More time to visit my mom, and my grandchildren and children.

Yoga. Maj. Book club. Lunch with friends.

Mixed media art class. Sharpening my computer skills. Mastering social media. Resurrection of my speaking career. A stab at publishing another book of my "Incidentally, Iris" columns. Setting up a website. Putting out a weekly newsletter.

Excitement bubbles up. Clearly, I will have the time to indulge my passions, expand my horizons and learn new things.

I give notice.

The first week home, I start where I always start when embarking on a new endeavor: I create order out of chaos. I clean out closets. And more closets. And the garage. And the back porch storage area. I line up my books neatly on the bookshelves that overshadow every room. I sweep crumpled papers and out-of-date notices off table tops. I toss out catalogs and magazines. I de-clutter the masses of dust-collecting knick-knacks. And cart the overage to the Salvation Army thrift store down the street.

Everything that needs fixing gets fixed. House plants get re-potted and fertilized. My wardrobe gets updated. I buy birthday presents way in advance and cook and freeze as if an avalanche of snow will be hitting Tampa Bay in a matter of hours.

And then, like a charging bull hitting a concrete wall, I become immobilized.

I plunk my tired body onto the couch and stay there. I watch the workers out of my backyard window construct two houses side by side, directly behind mine. I am thankful for the activity. I listen to the near constant traffic whizzing by my corner lot. And I am thankful for its muted low humming. I watch neighbors walking dogs. And gardeners mowing lawns. And repairmen fixing roofs. And arborists cutting limbs. I am thankful for their workday busyness. It lends normality to a world which is suddenly strange and intimidating to me.

I can feel ED's presence, peering around corners, beckoning me with a seductive gaze.

I catch myself wanting to flirt back.

My 24-Hour Day Now

Gradually, as I adapt to a "non-working" regimen, I go back to feeling comfortable with my home having the lived-in look.

My dining room table is once again filling up with my collage projects—half-finished, half-conceived.

My couch sports a long, rectangular basket filled to overflowing with magazines, articles of interest I intend to read, pencils, knitting needles, yarn and stitch counters, crochet hooks, hand lotion, magic markers and yellow highlighters, and colored paper clips and Kleenex.

Using my vegetable steamer. Learning about my slow cooker. Aiming to go back to outdoor grilling. Attend a juicing class. Buy a juicer. Still haven't used it.

Re-organizing my cookbooks by genre and keeping them in close sight. Tearing out recipes from magazines. Buying leeks for the first time. Growing basil by my porch.

My evenings are my own. No longer waging a raging internal debate over whether to binge and purge. Now free to relax or be productive.

I am on the inside what I always portrayed on the outside. Happy. Content. Appreciative. At peace. Grateful. Comfortable. Relaxed.

I stopped looking for a savior and I saved myself.

Getting in Touch With My Essence: Taking a Risk

What comes our way in life can be looked upon as an obstacle or an opportunity—an obstacle that blocks us, terrifies us, and stops us in our tracks or an opportunity for growth, renewal, and positive change.

A way to turn an obstacle into an opportunity is to take a risk. And author and trailblazer Erica Jong has something to say on this subject. (You may remember her for coining the phrase "the zipless f--k" in her book *Fear of Flying*, published in 1973.)

This is what she has to say about risk: "If you don't risk anything, you risk even more."

I recognize I did just that when I sought help with my bulimia, but I have also done that in more lighthearted ways.

Here's one of them I wrote about:

My friend Betty is a born flirt. She is playful, attentive, frothy and light, and men trip all over themselves to help pull out her chair, fetch her a drink, open her door.

The rest of us stand in awe. "How does she do it?" we ask ourselves. "And how can we get a little of what she's got?"

Being somewhat uninhibited, I am designated by my friends to be the one to ask Betty for her secret formula. I start out hesitantly, a little fearful that perhaps Betty will misconstrue my interest as criticism.

Betty instantly puts me at ease, casually throwing an arm around my shoulder and leaning in close. "The secret is a good marriage," she whispers. "A good marriage gives you confidence and the belief in yourself that you are a worthy person. And this confirmation comes from someone who knows you inside and out.

"My husband," continues Betty, "still loves me, reveres me and honors me in spite of my faults and shortcoming. Because of that, I feel tremendously valuable, confident and whole. Therefore I can flirt."

"Wait a minute," I said. "I don't get the connection."

"Look up flirting in the dictionary," Betty says lightly as she floats off to talk to her son's soccer coach.

I take her advice. Webster's says to flirt is to court triflingly or to act amorously without serious intentions.

Ah, I am starting to get it. The same skills she obviously employs with her husband, she carries out into the real world but playfully, without commitment or promise.

I call her cell phone. "Okay. Do it for fun. For frivolity. For laughs. But what if you come off like a bimbo? What if the guy has no sense of humor? What if you make a fool out of yourself?"

"Slow down," she cautions. "You are forgetting the Cardinal Rule of Flirting. You can't own the outcome. As long as you play loose, you're fine. Once you become concerned with how things will turn out, you are no longer flirting," she warns, "but courting disaster."

I go home to ponder her words.

I know I need some practice, but the building blocks are there.

I've got a good marriage and the confidence that comes from knowing that no matter how silly, immature, inappropriate and downright nasty I can sometimes act, my husband loves me. And can still somehow manage to see the good in me, even when none is being exhibited.

So I decide to practice on him. After all, I reason, if I make a jackass out of myself in front of him, it certainly won't be the first time. Or the last.

So I'm taking a few deep breaths and plunging into waters that have long been too tranquil. When he comes home from work, I'm holding in my stomach, smiling coquettishly, leaning up against him and running my hands playfully through his thinning hair.

Instead of asking him what his opinion is on the Iraqi war and the rising cost of homeowners insurance, I'm asking him what pleases him—what makes him happy, what he finds romantic.

He checks my forehead to see if I am running a fever. He checks the outside of the house to see if he has walked into the right one. And I realize that it's been too long since I've asked such questions.

When he sees that I am serious, he pauses and then says softly, "I think the most romantic thing is to see you smile. Your whole face lights up."

This time, I look at him to see if he is joking, but he's not. I start to glow. My eyelashes start to flutter. My hips start to sashay, my body moves closer to his.

I think I am getting it now.

Who knows? Today, my husband. Tomorrow, the world.

Getting in Touch With My Essence: Developing a Personal Mission Statement

I am exploring the realm of daring to be myself—of opening up new vistas of opportunity for myself, dreaming new dreams and implementing strategies to employ them. Daring to be myself—the best I can be. Reaching my full potential, attaining "gross profit" status and full operating capacity. That's uncharted territory for me.

Randomly searching the Internet one morning, I come across an article penned by a palliative care nurse, who works with patients the last three to twelve weeks of their lives. She questioned them about the regrets they had and what they would have done differently.

The common five responses are as follows:
- The courage to live a life true to myself
- The wish that I didn't work so hard
- The courage to express my feelings
- The wish to have stayed in touch more with my friends
- The wish to have let myself be happier

I need a way to asterisk this wisdom. It propels me to hunker down and develop a personal mission statement for myself. My mission statement will serve me as a set of rules, guidelines, and criteria—a source-book for keeping myself on track.

A mission statement is important because it works like a constitution. I can come back to it time and time again to keep myself on track. And I can amend it if need be. My mission statement will reflect WHO I AM, NOT WHAT I WANT TO DO. This is an important distinction. A very wise person once said, "People are not what they do. People are what they are. If we were what we did, we would be called human doings, not human beings." I keep that thought close.

Here's my mission statement:

My mission is to be the best that I can be, not being unduly ruled by the demands of time, energy and emotions placed on me by others. My objective is to assess each situation separately, being aware of my own needs, wants, limitations and feelings. My mission is to work and play with equal vigor—fully present in the moment—and to actively court happiness.

Getting in Touch With My Essence: Embracing the Past

I met the man who would become my second husband at our tenth high school reunion. We hadn't seen each other since graduation.

We got married one year later. Since then, our high school reunions are both highly anticipated and wrapped in swirls of emotions.

Our latest high school reunion was no different. I got ready for this reunion much like I got ready for my tenth reunion—in a hurry with the house a mess. Dressing while throwing in loads of dirty wash. Agonizing over my hips. Berating myself for not losing the five pounds I vowed I would the last time I saw these people. Worrying about what shenanigans the kids and their buddies would pull while I was out. Trying on four outfits before I am comfortable about how I look. And still not comfortable. Wondering about who else will be there. And who won't. And why.

My husband and I enter the large party room hand in hand. Masses of people mingling. Music blaring. Hugging. So many of us hugging. Squeals of delight. Whispered confessions. Huddles of three. Pushing. Back slapping. Hand holding. Snippets of so many sentences beginning with:

I know you won't believe this but....

Remember when....

Does your mom still...

I was always afraid to....

You were always...

So little talk on stocks to buy, candidates to vote for, foreign ports to visit, or new stores to shop.

I can't seem to articulate exactly what I feel so poignantly, so vividly, so deeply about my high school reunion experience. I know it's a marker of time passing that can't be denied. Of no longer being the rookies of the year. Of no longer dreaming of what we can be when we grow up. Because, we are grown up.

But this I know to be true:

I judge my high school classmates differently than I judge others. Less harshly. I love them for the very foibles and failings that in others I abhor.

My boyfriend will always be my boyfriend, no matter how long we've both been married to other people.

My best friend will always be my best friend, no matter how many other best friends I have made.

The ones who danced with abandon and delight all night long, still do. And the ones who hugged the sidelines watching everyone else laugh and whoop it up, still do.

We are past boasting.

Some of us live in our dream houses. Most of us are making do with what we've got.

Some of us had kids and some of us didn't. And for those that did, some of our high expectations were met and some were lowered.

How do I sum up a four-year experience that happened so long ago, but indelibly shaped me into the person I became, am capable of becoming and sometimes even rise to the occasion to become?

Barbra Streisand expressed it in the song, "The Way We Were."

"...Can it be that it was all so simple then?
Or has time re-written every line?
If we had the chance to do it all again
Tell me, would we? Could we?..."

One of my son Sam's closest friends said it just as well in fewer words when he called from college: "Life is great," he confided to Sam, "but I miss everybody."

ED wasn't there this time. And I didn't miss him.

Getting in Touch With My Essence: Blazing New Paths

As I distance myself from ED, I am realizing I need to blaze new paths. A friend of mine, Janet, was widowed at a young age. She picked up the pieces and went off and traveled on her own even though friends and relatives thought she was crazy.

Here are some excerpts from her first jaunt to Europe as a widow:

"For weeks preceding my trip, I remained on a euphoric high which unexpectedly came to a crashing halt the night of my departure at Kennedy Airport. Suddenly I was in the pits of depression. Sobbing tears sent streams of mascara cascading down my cheeks and the terribly chic merry widow totally dissolved. A nice lady from Chicago put a consoling arm around me and wondered why I was submitting myself to such torture. 'I have to prove to myself that I can do it,' I said. Boy, how I hated those trite words, but the mere fact that I had said them helped me regain my composure.

"Things went well for a while. I was doing just fine until we went down into the catacombs in Rome. In that awesome setting, my life began flashing before me again. I felt the presence of my husband and had the intense urge to light a candle in his memory.

"Soaring emotions overwhelmed me, and again the tears. And again that creepy thought: What on earth am I doing alone on the other side of the ocean? I recovered more rapidly from this cry and several of my newfound friends offered handkerchiefs and kindness.

"This first solo sojourn of mine, wrought with emotional highs and lows, was the turning point in my life. It totally changed my entire course of living. I acquired new friends, a new profession (travel writing) and a new outlook on life. Live while I'm alive. I even began to feel sorry for some of my complacent married friends who still thought it would go on forever."

I realize that when I dare to be myself and the best I can be, I also have to put up with the downside of things. I could be, like Janet, shedding a lot of tears—feeling very lonely at times—pushing myself almost to the point of exhaustion, past lethargy.

Is it worth the price to be paid?

I'm beginning to think it is.

Getting in Touch With My Essence: Getting Out of the Cage

A long time ago, Ann Kearney Cooke, founder and director of the Cincinnati Psychotherapy Institute and renowned for her research on eating disorders in young women, told me a short vignette:

There was a small town that had a zoo, and the people of the town wanted a polar bear, so the directors of the zoo raised the money to acquire a polar bear and build a habitat. The polar bear arrived early and so had to be confined in a cage until the habitat was finished.

When the habitat was ready, a ceremony took place to dismantle the cage and the polar bear was set free to explore his new living quarters—with all its nooks and crannies. But the polar bear kept moving as if the cage were still there.

"How many of us," Dr. Kearney-Cooke then asked me, "don't get out of the cages of our own making? How many of us are doomed to get the same disappointing results because we confine ourselves to the same limited space? How many of us hold onto outdated visions and unrealistic goals?"

I ask myself: If I am paralyzed by habit and indecision, what can I do to move myself forward?

I answer myself. I can embrace the adage of DOING ONE THING EVERY SINGLE DAY THAT SCARES ME.

Jerry Seinfeld says that it's a well-known fact that the number one fear people have is the fear of public speaking, followed by the fear of death. That means, Jerry surmises, that people attending a funeral would rather be the person in the casket than be the person delivering the eulogy!

I could relate to that! Public speaking was my nemesis.

After publishing my first book, *Slices, Bites and Other Facts of Life*, and enjoying a long run as a slice-of-life columnist, invitations to speak started rolling in. I was terrified.

What helped dispel the fear?

- Knowledge and research of my subject
- Thorough preparation
- Repetition and practice of my delivery
- Belief that I could indeed do it

Come to think of it, all of the above are also helping me overcome my dependence and attachment on ED and the cage in which he kept me.

Making Better Choices

My adult children get busier at their jobs, with more responsibilities.

They get busier at their lives with significant others, wives, and children of their own.

The lengthy phone calls dwindle dramatically.

More texts, but shorter ones.

Less frequent too.

And sometimes, they don't answer back at all.

Are they mad?

Uncaring?

Detached?

Is it that they love me less and need me little?
Or, is it as they purport? "Just really busy, Mom."
I wisely choose to assume the latter.

Walking with Stella

Okay, so I'm not a groupie. I'm not part of a lunch-bunch, a weekly card club or an ongoing theater group. I abhor clothes shopping with friends, traveling with other couples, hanging on the phone chit-chatting.

I am a loner.

Consistent with this preference, when I decided to incorporate into my routine a daily, hour and fifteen-minute killer walk, I chose to do it without company. My Sony Walkman and I were the best of buddies. And as long as my batteries were strong, I preferred to listen to oldies, books on tape or National Public Radio while I swayed, pushed, pulled and heaved my resistant body through a three and a half-mile trek.

It's not that I haven't been asked by various friends over the years to walk. It's just that I never felt the need nor desire to conform to someone else's erratic schedule. And think about this: Committing seventy-five minutes a day to talking to the same person is a huge investment of time and energy. Especially when you aren't even married to that person.

The first couple of times Stella asked me to walk, I resisted. Until finally, one day, I relented—somewhat reluctantly and apprehensively, I must admit.

Besides from just picking a convenient time for both of us, I obsessed over the pace. There is nothing more aggravating to a Type A personality than having to slow down her pace to accommodate another. And who walks on the outside, and who walks on the inside, and who has the final say on the route we follow? It all seemed too complicated for me.

In retrospect, I should have conserved my energy in order to keep up with Stella's killer pace. And I must admit I quickly learned that when you are having a good, old-fashioned heart-to-heart conversation, the route, the time, the weather, the position and the place become secondary to the content.

Sometime in that first couple of weeks of walking together, a profound change occurred. And I began to understand what all my friends who walk together had been telling me for years: IT'S CHEAPER THAN THERAPY AND MORE FUN.

So I asked Arlene—who just happens to be a social worker heading a big agency in town—about that off-the-top-of-my-head theory, and here is what she said. "I like to believe therapy is more than walking. However, walking with friends is a wonderful way to reduce stress, solve problems, get advice, and just vent. And I would hope the advice may include the suggestion to seek therapy if necessary."

Sherry, an attorney, says walking isn't a replacement for therapy, but it's a close second, providing her a way to unwind and regroup at the end of the day. "I have been walking with the same two women night after night, five to six days every week, for over ten years. At three miles a night, that's close to 9,000 miles—and a lot of conversation. It is an integral part of my life."

Karen says walking is better than therapy. "You don't have to spend the whole walk consumed with 'therapy' issues. You can get it off your chest, reflect, gain another perspective and then spend the rest of the time commenting on the landscaping and decorating accomplishments (and failings) along your route."

So Stella and I walk, every day—rain, shine, darkness or light. We have covered all the stuff you would expect two women past their childbearing years to cover—old boyfriends, first husbands, second husbands, kids, hairdos and weight.

As the days roll by, our comfort level increases and the depth of our conversation expands. We start off with banter to re-establish the groove and by the time we round the first corner, we are off to another round of jabbering and interacting that doesn't end until we come to my driveway and part for the day.

Sloppy ruminations. Judgmental quips. Rambling observations. As another friend, Lisa, says, "It's a non-threatening way of un-burdening oneself."

We also have become accountable to each other. I tell her I won't walk with her on Thursday unless she applies for the part-time position she has been talking about for the last ten days. She tells me what I need to do to prevent shin splints and yellow teeth, and which vitamins I should be taking, while issuing a deadline for compliance. We seem to buoy each other up, calm each other down and hold each accountable in order to encourage the other to be the best and most productive she can be.

Sagacious Margie states that starting the day with a walk has saved many a day from going downhill before the day even begins. And Julie, known for her spunk and creativity, further confides that, "A walking partner is like BRAN in your diet. Your partner keeps you REGULAR."

Stella and I have never discussed it but I think we both have come to acknowledge and embrace the unwritten rule of walking buddies. We leave on the sidewalk what we have covered in conversation that day. It never makes it to the dinner table in our homes. Call it confidentiality in the walk place.

It's been an integral part of my recovery.

ED's in a Safe Silo, or Is He?

Things are going well.
   I get weighed once a month.
   And I track my points.
   The days pass.

I catch up on my reading.

Travel to see my mom and grandkids.

I sign up for a webinar on social media and publishing for authors.

I'm overwhelmed with new information. Dazzled by possibility.

I make the decision to write about ED.

I begin with the events leading up to me seeking treatment.

Writing fills my free time, occupies my thoughts.

And it keeps ED in a safe place—the past.

Then my husband gets sick.

My legs turn into noodles.

My brain stops processing.

My heart pounds incessantly.

My mind can't comprehend what the doctors are telling me.

But, like I did at age seven, according to my mom, when my beloved grandmother got cancer and died within weeks, I slid into "coping mode" and "never missed a beat."

And my writing stops abruptly.

Immediate Halt

My life, as I know it, comes to an immediate halt.

Unbeknownst to my husband and me, an insidious bacterial infection was slowly sweeping its way through his body, destroying everything in its path. It would eat away a major portion of his vertebrae and wreak havoc with his brain.

My alpha male, my perennial rookie of the year, a lifelong bodybuilder, was reduced to a state of what the doctors would later describe as "temporarily totally disabled."

It was a life-altering diagnosis, stemming from an epidural abscess—an abscess that took months to discover and additional months to isolate. It was probably contracted through a less-than-sterile epidural steroid procedure performed in a doctor's office.

I became the alpha advocate. His caretaker extraordinaire. My days became a maze of hospital visits, rehab units and outpatient care.

His gym bag was replaced by canes and walkers in our front hall. A handicapped sticker hung from my car as I chauffeured him to and from a dizzying array of doctor appointments. He was treated in public with deference and sympathy. He was enraged by the looks of pity.

We no longer went for walks, because he couldn't cover more than a mere twelve feet.

We no longer went to art fairs, planned day trips or attended concerts.

We bided our time—patiently and impatiently—watching his incision close, his limp recede, his stamina increase.

And then came days of de-stabilization. And maddening regression.

Most days ED kept his distance, respectful of our plight. I didn't see him at all, but thought of him intermittently—as I stepped out of the shower into my empty bedroom early in the morning, readying to face another grueling day at the hospital with my husband. As I ate dinner alone watching the nightly news. When I perused the grocery aisles shopping for one. When I searched for a caretaker for when my husband returned home. When I navigated the maze of hospital forms and insurance claims.

Some days I glimpsed ED casually leaning on the doorpost of my husband's hospital bed, observing the scene of IV tubes. Or lurking in the corridor as, tired and discouraged, I made my way to the elevator. Or following me to the parking lot, waving madly—trying to get my attention—as I fumbled with my keys.

One day, he almost made direct contact. I was sitting in a dimly-lit room in the intensive care unit early in the morning—perhaps two a.m.—watching my husband sleep fitfully. The surgeon, who would be operating first thing the next morning, had just departed for the hospital sleep room, after telling me there was a chance my husband's legs could remain in a floppy state. Paralyzed and useless. ED and I had a short exchange that night—while I visited the nearby vending machines and pulled the lever on three candy bars. Gobbling them down, I turned to see ED with hands outstretched, beckoning me to come closer for a hug. I pushed ED away and ran for the sanctuary of the ICU unit.

ED was my jilted boyfriend, my spurned lover, my rejected suitor. And I prayed I had the inner fortitude to keep him that way.

Reading in a Time of Upheaval

I branch out of my normal pattern of recreational reading and delve into the mystery genre. After one week of re-reading the first three chapters of my new mystery book four times, I abandon it for chick-lit. A health crisis calls for fantasy and romance, not noir themes of drugs, betrayal and murder.

ED taunts me, casually leaning over my shoulder as I restlessly flip the pages.

Looking Back

Looking back, it's clear I was not honest in regard to my ongoing attraction, attachment and loyalty to ED. I never even obliquely alluded to him in any aspect of my creative work—my weekly columns, my book, my speeches, my radio program. I was very honest, though, when it came to writing about most of the other facets of my life. I used my "Incidentally, Iris" column to expose my foibles, my fears and my frustrations. My weekly ruminations also charted my progress on many fronts—progress that at times led to victory and at times ended in disaster. The whimsical tone of my column and the humor-wrapped tales of my suburban, baby-boomer life flagged my triumphs and challenges. They documented life lessons learned from milestones, transitions and passages. As one astute observer commented, "Iris gives her readers broccoli, but she saturates it with cheese sauce."

Looking back, in some very elementary way, my columns themselves actually did enable me to "Keep Coping." I wrote about the untidy, aggravating, frustrating and sad parts of parenting, marriage, friendship, work, and household responsibilities. I wrote about the unexpected joys of family life and the sweet moments of repose, rest and rejuvenation that life also offered. The act of writing about these intimate experiences in such a straightforward manner kept the lid on the smoldering pot of my bulimia. Writing let out the steam, allowing the cauldron of my swirling emotions to keep simmering—without boiling over and creating untold chaos.

Lessons Learned Along the Way

Within minutes of Nelson Mandela's death in early December 2013, we are deluged with information about his life. He was a conqueror of apartheid, the first black president of South Africa, a master compromiser and a champion peace broker. One facet of his multi-layered life particularly fascinates me: How did he emerge from twenty-seven years of wrongful imprisonment devoid of bitterness and rancor? Myriad sources cite Mandela's anger in his early years of confinement. As time passed, however, Mandela noted that he began to recognize that "hating clouds the mind and gets in the way of strategy" (*The New York Times*, December 6, 2013). If he wanted to achieve lifelong dreams and ambitions, he realized he needed to control what was still left for him to control—his heart, his head, his thoughts and his attitude—or his captors would have indeed triumphed. Nelson Mandela entered prison as a revolutionary and emerged as a statesman.

I wonder how much time we all spend in a cell of our own making—raging about things we can't control, rather than concentrating on strategies that will strengthen our wills and help achieve our desired results?

Clearly I am stuck in neutral, trying to keep from unraveling as my husband's health continues to decline. Boxed into a caretaking role I was not prepared for, nor capable of fully and effectively embracing.

Perhaps I should think about shifting gears like author Cheryl Strayed. Reeling from the loss of her beloved mother, her life at age twenty-two was spiraling downward. Her family had fragmented and scattered. She was dabbling in heroin and free sex, estranged from her husband and employed in a series of dead-end jobs. In a desperate attempt to cure her of herself, Strayed decided that hiking the Pacific Crest Trail alone—from the Mojave Desert through California and Oregon to Washington—would be her path to salvation. That walking with no discernible reason, but just to observe the wonders of nature, would prove restorative. Years later, she documented her journey in *Wild*, a book gracing *The New York Times* Best Seller List for over thirty-five weeks.

Strayed documents how she suffered from her inexperience: not budgeting enough money to adequately see her through from outpost to outpost. She ignores admonishments about weighty backpacks, neglects to talk to anyone who has actually hiked the trail before her, and does woefully little physical training to prepare her for the rigors the trek will present. She encounters desert heat, frigid mountain air, rattlesnakes, eroded trails and a near rape from a lusty, lecherous mountain man. She endures massive foot blisters, bruising, hunger, thirst, exhaustion and loneliness.

Among her many notable trials and triumphs on the trail, I am most drawn to one part of it: the beginning. She wakes up the morning she is to start her journey in a seedy, cheap motel, twelve miles from the trail. She has trouble even lifting her backpack to position it across her back. And when she finally maneuvers that feat, she is already exhausted. Nevertheless, she closes the motel room door and steps into a parking light drenched in daylight. She realizes quickly—with great trepidation—that she is going to have to hitch a ride with strangers unless she wants to walk the twelve miles to the trail's entrance in the searing heat of a June day. Two men in a minivan with Colorado plates offer her a ride. She climbs in gingerly, hoping she won't get murdered. Thirty uneventful minutes later, they drop her off on a silent highway. She begins walking toward a fencepost supporting a palm-sized sign reading "Pacific Crest Trail." She staggers the first few steps down the trail. She finds the trail register in a metal box nearby and signs it. She resumes walking.

Her journey had begun. There were no crowds heaving fistfuls of graffiti. No cheering loved ones throwing kisses. No photographers eagerly snapping pictures documenting her first steps. No massive send-off parade. It was just an ordinary day in an ordinary town, as she took her first tentative steps off the highway and into the wilderness. And though the beginning was neither dramatic nor pain-free, she emerged at the end of her trek an altered person.

Like Cheryl Strayed, I vowed in the new year of 2014, to push myself to take those first faltering baby steps—as subtle and unnoticed by others as they may be—so that I can begin to achieve what really matters to me.

Like Nelson Mandela, in the new year of 2014, I would resolve to work diligently on strategies for achieving what I want in life. And give less credence to the wrongs heaped upon me.

Health Is Generally Good

I remember seeing a harried mother in the grocery store, yelling at her kids. And I swore I would never do that. Until I became a mother.

I remember seeing tired, grumpy, frumpy people walking hospital corridors, and I swore that if I ever had a loved one in the hospital, I'd make a supreme effort to be forever and at all times rested, upbeat and perfectly attired. Until my husband spent seventeen straight days in the hospital.

At first when my husband became a patient, I meticulously coordinated my outfits every morning before driving to the hospital. Black boots with four-inch heels, carefully applied makeup, sleek and shiny hair, and jewelry complementing every outfit. Topped off, of course, by my unblemished and professionally shellacked bright red nails.

The boots were the first to go, followed in rapid succession by my coordinated outfits, jewelry, makeup and hair. And the shellacked nails were picked off bit by bit the morning Steven had surgery. Three harrowing days into my husband's hospital stay, my hair was back to its naturally curly wild mess, and my face—unadorned and without blush, lipstick, foundation and mascara—looked pasty, pale and blemished. If that sad state of disrepair wasn't enough, my jeans went from loose to snug—a casualty of the carb binges I was indulging in nightly. (I envy people who stop eating under stress and lose tons of weight. Please don't share your stories with me, as it would only depress me more.)

You can tell a lot about a person by the first thing they read in the newspaper each day—whether in print or online. One of my biggest luxuries is reading *The New York Times* delivered to my door each Sunday morning. The Sunday Style section is the first section I turn to and the Modern Love column the first thing I read. On the second Sunday of my husband's hospital stay, I read about the editor of the Modern Love column remarking on the kind of submissions he gets—those asking how they find love and those asking how they get it back.

My husband and I have been married thirty-seven years and, though we occasionally enjoy moments of exquisite passion, I would have to characterize our long-term marriage as one where "good enough is great." We are what the Modern Love columnist would term "the appreciatively resigned." We rise each morning not dwelling on our marital shortfalls but counting our mutual blessings...managing over the years to "grow together rather than apart." When describing these couples, columnist Daniel Jones notes that their health is "generally good."

Ah, the operative phrase: their health is generally good. Enjoying good health—not even great health—is clutch. Having a critically ill spouse, my perspective shifts and my gratification meter ticks wildly in a whole new direction. I forget about how annoying he is when he leaves his gym shoes by my side of the bed each night, and I unfailingly trip over them at three a.m. while hurrying to void my post-menopausal bladder. Instead, I hope one day soon to marvel anew at the happy coincidence that when I get up in the middle of the night, he gets up too—once again reminding me just how in sync our body rhythms are.

And instead of impatiently counting the minutes until he flies down the stairs once again fifteen minutes late for a dinner date with friends, I wonder if he will ever wean himself from the walker and come flying down the stairs unaided again—whether on time or late. And as one hospital day bleeds into the next, I find myself immersed in counting other things besides how many minutes late he is. I now compulsively keep track of blood pressure numbers, temperature readings, white blood counts, laps walked around the hospital corridor, calories eaten and food left on his plate. I confer with his team of doctors, search the Internet for background medical information, ply my physician friends with questions and monitor his daily doings. I am now firmly entrenched as his alpha advocate.

It would be trite to say I am overwhelmingly grateful for the possibility that within a few months we can return to our normal—and sometimes annoying and sometimes uneventful—routine. But it would be true.

Foray into Escapism

My next foray into escapism involves skin care. I figure maybe I can allay the rampant ravages of stress attacking my blotchy face and regain some rosiness. My daughter-in-law's friend—a bona fide skin care specialist—recommends an array of actions to preserve what is left of my quickly fading bloom. Exfoliating daily. Eating plenty of avocados. Juicing. Staying hydrated. Professional facials. And checking out skin-care websites such as Dermalogica.com.

Information overload strikes quickly. The whole skin care scene is simply too daunting to navigate at this point. Forgoing my nightly diet orange soda and instead gulping down eight ounces of bottled water is all I can manage at this point.

Along with ignoring ED's pleas for a reconciliation.

The Caramel Caper

I buy bags of caramels, individually wrapped, at a local discount store.

I buy them for two reasons. First, my husband loves them as a pop-in-your-mouth-while-watching-sports-on-the-big-screen-TV snack. And second, I love them because their rich butterscotch color matches my couch. No kidding. They blend in so well with my decorating scheme that most of the time I forget they are there—just a few footsteps away from me.

For days, I pass the stash of caramels with nary a thought. But sometimes, late at night, particularly when my eyelids are heavy and my defenses down, the caramels exude their spell on my sleepy-time body. I get reeled in like a fisherman reels in his catch of the day. First, I grab a bunch of the cellophane wrapped wonders. I slowly unwrap the candy and pop two of them at the same time into my mouth. Carefully smoothing the square of caramel into a flat large surface with my tongue, I savor the gooey sweetness and suck away. I swallow and pop a few more into my mouth before climbing the center hall stairs to my bed.

This routine goes on for weeks. Until my next Weight Watchers weigh-in, to be precise. The scale's number reflects a four-pound weight gain. It is truly a WTF moment.

"How can this be?" I screech to myself. Clearly, it's time for a caramel candy reckoning.

I arrive home and immediately tear through the garbage for the bag the caramels come in. I double click on my Weight Watchers app on my iPhone and scan the bar code to determine the number of points in each caramel.

Oy.

There is no quibbling with the bar scanner. Each caramel I have been casually popping in my mouth registers as one full point. I have been accumulating approximately ten points at each sitting. It doesn't take a math genius to quickly calculate that if I allow myself a total of twenty-five Weight Watcher points per day max to maintain my weight, I am eating over one-third of my allotted points in caramels alone. No wonder my hips now carry a wad of extra padding.

Maybe the adage "out of sight out of mind" is really effective. Maybe I should ditch the caramels and switch to peppermints? They are red and white—also blending beautifully with the surroundings—and they are hard candy with fewer calories. And, when tired, how could I have the energy to suck more than a few before the roof of my mouth gets scratchy and I fall asleep from the sheer effort of sucking and swallowing?

Caramels proved just too tempting to keep on the end table beside the couch. Once again the lesson learned is to remove the temptation.

Sorry, Steven. As I see it you have two choices: develop a taste for peppermint or keep the caramels in your pocket.

To Be Perfectly Honest

To be perfectly honest, I was feeling quite sorry for myself. My husband's road to recovery had been bumpier than anticipated. I was struck down with a killer sinus infection that disrupted our already meager weekend plans we had managed to pull together. And one of our best couple friends was moving to Maine.

My usual positive frame of mind had abandoned me. I was falling into an abyss of negativism.

I began flipping through my arsenal of Pollyannaish phrases in an effort to banish the blues. The first one springing to mind was the tried and true "count your blessings" mantra. "Nope," I said to myself emphatically, "I'm sick of that worn-out phrase." So I kept searching for a more effective panacea as I roamed my house—my very cherished and carefully tended house, that through my efforts and my husband's willingness, reflected our family history, our tastes, our values and our lifestyle.

But the anemic phrase "count your blessings" followed me as I scrambled eggs for breakfast in my favorite non-stick pan, while watching the morning news on my readily accessible flat screen smart TV. Later in the day, I Skyped with two of my grandchildren and then carefully tended my masses of riotously blooming house plants. Still in a funk, I desultorily fetched the mail, making a mental note to deposit the short-term disability check my husband had received, and to check my bank balance to see if our Social Security check had arrived. Poor me.

I wandered into my book-lined living room. I stumbled upon the box of family photos I had dumped out while looking for the perfect ones to assemble for a sign-in board for my youngest son's thirtieth birthday party—a party I would be attending in New York City the following weekend. Poor, poor me.

And that is when I started thinking about what other people had written about their lives and blessings.

Sarah Breathnach, author of *Simple Abundance*, a day book of comfort and joy, focuses on savoring the smallest details, rather than that which is lacking in her life. The daisies in a jar on the windowsill. The fragrance of a child or grandchild's hair. The first sip of coffee in the morning. When we can't access our inner resources to empower ourselves to feel happy and fulfilled, Breathnach advises us to focus on the abundance in our lives. And gratitude is the key.

In *Chestnut Street*, Maeve Binchy's collection of short stories published posthumously, Binchy cites a character named Molly, who is seeking a cure for her sleeplessness. She is advised to do the following:

Buy a big notebook with at least twenty pages in it. Stick a picture on the cover, something to do with flowers. On the night you can't sleep, get up and dress as if going out visiting. Make a cup of tea, get out the notebook and, in your best handwriting, write about just one thing that makes you happy. Then spend a whole hour doing something you had meant to do, like polishing the silver or arranging photographs in an album. Then undress carefully and go back to bed.

At the end of the twenty days, Molly realized that her life was more organized, her sleeping was more satisfying and there were still so many more blessings she hadn't written about.

No matter how you present it, quantifying what is good in your life works. It works for authors, sages and the common man. And I am going to remember that when the going gets rough, my scale tips high and my spirits sag. As my friend Damon, the plumber, wisely noted in a text he sent me last week about his life, "I continue to look for the right choices, accept what my present circumstances are. I don't focus on the problem. I search instead for the possibilities. And I dedicate my life to a celebration of renewal and change."

The Talmud tells us that we will be called on to account for every permissible pleasure life offered us, but which we refused to enjoy while on Earth. So here's to both joyfulness and mindfulness. And fewer caramels.

730 Days without ED

February 14, 2014.

It's been two years since I have binged and purged.

I buy another piece of jewelry from the boutique in the mall specializing in watches, bracelets, rings and necklaces handcrafted in Spain.

This time I select a multi-strand bracelet that drapes loosely around my wrist. The entwining suede ropes are brown and the beads are multi-colored. The frame is silver.

Three hundred sixty-five dollars for another three hundred six-ty-five days without ED.

I put it on before leaving the store.

Tripping the Smell Fantastic

I don't know whether it was laziness, frugality or political correctness (deferring to those unfortunate souls with allergies), but I stopped wearing perfume after college. Now that I think about it, ED didn't like it. The only sensory pleasure he gave me permission to indulge in was the sense of taste. Not smell. He was adamant.

But ED is no longer around.

So it's no wonder that my stash of fragrances has become markedly depleted. Upon taking inventory, I was appalled to glean this hard stat: only one half-filled bottle of Chanel No. 5 graced my dressing table.

Embarking on manic and gargantuan organizing sprees is one way I mange stress. With my husband's current state of health still classified as "under the weather," I, with wild abandon, embarked on a cleaning-out-my-closets binge. Tidying and sorting and streamlining my messy cubbyholes brought a much-needed sense of order and control to my physical environment.

My first frenzied foray centered on my hall linen closet. By the time I had re-folded and re-stacked the last bath towel in the linen closet, a pile of thirty-one sample bottles of perfume lay at my feet. The identifying names on the vials had long ago faded, but the fragrances appeared to be still intact, so they were spared the undignified fate of landing in the box destined for the Salvation Army.

So the very next morning—and every morning that followed— before setting out for the hospital to visit my husband, I capriciously picked a vial, sprayed liberally in appropriate and not-so-appropriate places, and headed out the door. And without fail, each morning as

I hugged my husband hello, he smiled broadly and told me yet again how great I smelled.

Clearly, I was onto something.

The days rolled by with little resolution of my husband's medical situation. As my frustration mounted, so did the amount of perfume I liberally poured on daily. Soon my stash of sample fragrances was sorely depleted too. Buoyed by my husband's enthusiastic reaction to my newly fragranced presence, I began to re-think my grooming routine and decided to add perfume to my morning regimen. This called for good, old-fashioned retail therapy.

One evening, when sleep eluded me once again, I whipped out my iPad and boldly typed in "perfume."

First I researched my mom's favorite, Odalisque, named after a concubine in a Turkish harem in the household of an ottoman Turk. Released in 1946 by a nice Jewish lady, Nettie Rosenstein, its scent was too floral to be considered a sex bomb perfume, but did manage to express the complex femininity of the 1950s, thus becoming wildly popular, though pricey.

Next I read about prostitutes and courtesans who, on the other hand, tended to favor the sexually provocative fragrances heavy with animal musk or jasmine. Coco Chanel was savvy enough to combine both, launching Chanel No. 5 in the era of the liberated flapper. It's my favorite.

Deep into the night, I stumbled on a site profiling "The Ten Perfumes with the Longest Lasting Scents." I was captivated. I decided to treat myself to two of those listed. But which ones?

Comparative shopping proved difficult. First of all, although I could read lengthy entries describing each perfume in precise detail and clearly see a listing of each ingredient, I had no idea whatsoever of how each perfume smelled. And I was totally confused between cologne, perfume, toilet water, sprays, etc. Shipping options furthered muddled the mess. But, as the sun broke over the eastern horizon, I had narrowed my search down to two:

Cinema by Yves St. Laurent

Infusion d'Iris by Prada.

I sheepishly admit I picked the latter solely due to its name, but the ingredients tantalized too: incense, cedar and iris. Cinema sported jasmine, conjuring up images of me adorned in high heels and black, seamed stockings. I figured introducing a little raciness in my life was a good thing.

So, at present, I am busy tracking my purchases, anxiously anticipating arrival of the olfactory. My husband and I are still waiting for things to resolve medically. But at least for now, I know that each and every morning I will be greeted by a smiling husband because, quite simply, I will just smell so damn good.

Ha ha, ED.

Tree Care as a Metaphor for Self Care

The days drag on. My husband remains in convalescent mode. Well-meaning friends pull me aside to tell me I look tired. Bone tired. No kidding?

I try to distract myself from the weariness.

Diversion and direction come from an unexpected source: a tall, middle-aged husky fellow with a full beard, attired in flannel shirt, ripped jeans, combat boots and a straw cowboy hat perched precariously on his head. He came knocking on my door and convinced me that my grand oaks were in need of his services. I was an easy sell. We've lived here eight years—all without maintaining those majestic wonders.

I checked out his credentials and gave the go-ahead.

While his crew spends six hours re-invigorating my trees—pruning trimming, cutting, and fertilizing—he educates me on the proper care of these living organisms.

He points out a tree trunk with a lost limb. "Long ago, this limb had been removed properly," he remarks. "It was causing undue stress on the rest of the tree. Because this limb has been removed properly, the tree will completely heal and close around the wound. If the scar does not heal properly, water sets in the cavity and, after a time, will slowly rot the inside of the trunk."

He looks at me intently and continues. "It's okay to have scars. They just must heal properly.

"Look up at the canopy of limbs overhead," he instructs me. "It's important to clean out the sucker limbs so that the wind can blow freely through and the tree won't topple when in the eye of a storm. Suckers catch the wind and take nutrients from the rest of the tree, especially the tree tops."

He looks at me intently again. "It's okay to allow for some hangers-on, but too many suckers will cause the tree to die.

"One more thing." He looks back over his shoulder as he climbs into the cab of his truck. "The size of the canopy gives a suggestion of the size of the tree's surface roots. Take care of the roots—they are reputed to hold all the tree's strength."

I head back to my husband's rehab room refreshed, energized and more hopeful than I have felt in days. Trees are living organisms that naturally know how to survive. We humans should take a few clues and cues from them:

- Allow ourselves to heal from within, not with a quick outer fix
- Shed the excess baggage to lighten our load
- Honor and draw strength from our roots, the part of us that holds our power and potency

And don't be reluctant to take advice from a weathered, bearded arborist who draws beautiful metaphors between caring for trees and surviving life's perils.

Play

Just for one day, I am turning my back on my arthritic knees, the power and worth of networking, the overabundance of unpaid bills, and the presence of a dirty refrigerator emitting a noxious odor. Just for one day, I am calling a moratorium on work, writing, straightening messy closets, and finishing partially completed projects, no matter how worthy.

I am going to play. For years, my only "playmate" was ED. Now, the scope and breadth of my playing field is dizzying. Ripe with possibility.

I am going to think about style, not substance. I am shamelessly going to work on the outside of me, not the inside. And I'm going to sleep late, not just on Saturday, but on a Thursday too. And have my mom call and cancel all my work-related activities, explaining that I'm home sick with a stomachache.

Just for one day, I want to re-awaken the kid I was. I want macaroni and cheese for lunch, not steamed veggies. I want to have milk and cookies at four o'clock, not six ounces of fat-free, artificially sweetened yogurt. I want meatloaf for dinner, not grilled salmon steaks. And I want someone else to cook it.

Not surprisingly, reports that an especially strong wave of childishness in adults began surfacing about two years ago, with more and more baby boomers seeking comfort in childhood attachments and childhood/adolescent behaviors in an attempt to ameliorate the jitters following 9/11.

So I'm not alone. It's not just globally disturbing catastrophes that are awakening "the kid" in many of us. It's career disappointments. Flawed relationships. Errant children. Maxed-out credit. Lumpy bodies. Adulthood has lost its rapturous appeal, and the Peter Pan attitude is making great inroads into the way we map out our days and spend our disposable income and free time.

And marketers are starting to pay attention to "re-juveniles"—those adults with busy lives, responsible jobs, and children of their own, who want to recapture the fun of growing up. These men and women seek out accoutrements that either accompanied that rite of passage or continue to symbolize a fun-filled, flexible, lively lifestyle.

Thinking of replacing my aging station wagon, my kids offer suggestions. The unanimous choice for me was a four-door sedan with seat warmers and computer-programmed windshield wipers.

I scoff at their selection. It's so predictable. I don't want to give up my individuality and sense of adventure just because I'm well past fifty.

"How about the new Honda Element?" I query. They look at me like I've lost my mind.

"Mom, that's for kids who live in dorms and surf the oceans."

Interesting enough, I learn that the average age of Element drivers, according to a spokesman for the American Honda Motor Company, is forty—well above the age of those who are housed in university quarters.

I am spurred on.

"Well, how about a jet-black PT Cruiser with a big purple iris painted on the driver's door?" I ask my sons the next time they are gathered around my kitchen table. And even though I am greeted with horrified silence, I mentally make a note to look up custom car painters in the yellow pages.

Just for one day, I want to re-capture my own inner child. I want to hang out with my friends who knew me before push-up bras replaced cotton undershirts. I want to while away the afternoon playing jacks and Crazy Eights, making root beer floats, and flopping on my unmade bed to listen to Dion and the Belmonts. I want to talk about boys, trade lipsticks, and try on my friends' spike heels. I want to rest my chin in the palm of my hand, sit cross-legged on the floor, close my eyes, and imagine how it would feel to be kissed by a well-muscled beach boy. I want to jitterbug and do the stroll. And gorge myself on M&Ms and buttered popcorn—without once counting calories and carbs or thinking about my high cholesterol.

Just for one day, I will ignore thoughts of dry rot and deteriorating roof shingles, inching up mortgage rates, and broken vacuum cleaners.

Just for one day, I will live gloriously, heedlessly, abundantly and happily. I will welcome back the magnetism of my youth and carry it over into my slumber. I will dream of all of life's endless possibilities and then wake up with the wherewithal and energy to make my dreams come true.

Down Day

I just found a quick fix for a down day.

Do a Google search for "25 funniest auto correct mistakes ever."

Here's a sample:

Ah, the Kids

I have five sons—Harry, Frank, Max, Sam, Louie—all now adults.

When they were still at home and occupying chairs around the wooden kitchen table, if they saw me overeat, they never commented.

If they saw me excuse myself from the dinner table and return a few minutes later with red knuckles and a flushed face, they never questioned my short absence and altered appearance.

If they knew about my bizarre nightly routine after they went to bed, they gave no indication—overt or otherwise.

I spent their growing-up years actively bulimic. But I believe they were unknowing.

I wanted to be for them the rock I believed they needed, even if I couldn't be that rock for myself. A note my son Max sent to me years later, in 2010, brought great comfort.

Dear Mom,

Although as one of the bros, we collectively got you what I hope you think are good gifts, I did not want Mother's Day to go by without me expressing to you what a good mother I think you are.

As a child, I always felt that you were steadfastly by my side and always had my best interest at heart during tough times. As I continue to move down the parenting continuum, I become aware of all things that you did and for that I want to offer my sincerest thanks as I know it was probably not always easy.

Happy Mother's Day.

Love,
Max

Tackling the Task of Telling the Kids

Telling my kids about my bulimia was not going to be like an easy ride around the block. My friend and fellow sufferer, Joy—who has four kids and had been bulimic for almost as long as I had—assured me that they already knew.

"No way," I shot back at her, over lunch one day. "I hid it very well. And quite honestly, my boys had and have very little interest in the minutiae of my life."

"This isn't minutiae," Joy curtly replied.

On that I had to agree.

I decided to broach the subject to my sons in their chronological birth order. I started with Harry, who at the time was in his early forties, single and living nearby. I called him up and asked him to lunch—prefacing it with the statement, "I have something I want to share with you.

"Really," I berated myself silently, right after adding that superfluous last phrase. "Was it necessary to add more drama to an already emotionally laden situation?"

After we ordered, I leaned in close, took a deep breath and began. "Harry, I want you to know I have been fighting a demon for most of my life. Since I was eighteen, I have been bulimic."

There was dead silence. And then rumbles of unrestrained laughter burst forth from Harry.

Of all the reactions I had prepared myself to expect, unreserved mirth was not on the docket.

"How utterly insensitive," I seethed, throwing him a cold, glowering stare.

"Mom," he replied earnestly, "I'm not laughing at your being bulimic. I would never do that. I'm laughing because it's so typical of something you would do."

"Something I would do?" I repeated, clearly still puzzled.

"Well," Harry said in a matter of fact tone, "it seems like you have forgotten, but you already confessed this to me, years ago, when I was in college."

Now it was my turn to laugh.

During dessert, I brought him up to date, filling in my timeline in a generalized manner: vowing to stop bingeing and purging, seeking outpatient treatment, going three times weekly, learning how to re-orient my thoughts and actions, learning to practice the concept of mindful eating and resolute action.

After deliberating mightily, I decided to skip my next two oldest sons. Because they were both married, it made things more complicated.

I jumped next to Sam, at the time approaching the age of thirty, reluctantly residing with us after graduating from law school. After my revelation about seeking treatment, he seemed relieved. "I knew you were going someplace after work, but I couldn't figure out where. So that clears up the mystery. Way to go, Mom."

My youngest son, Lou, was the next recipient of my confession. Lou at the time was in his late twenties, living in New York City, dating a lovely young woman whom he had met at the law firm where they both worked. His brothers referred to him jokingly as "the daughter I never had." He was sensitive, openly affectionate and always responded in an endearing, sympathetic manner to whatever tale I was imparting.

I called him on the phone, but took a different approach, reciting my tale in a calm, straightforward manner, with minimal fanfare.

"I want you to know that for forty-six years I have been bulimic, Lou. I went for treatment and I haven't binged nor purged in nineteen months."

"Wow, Mom, that's a lot to take in. I knew girls in high school that had that problem. "

Mirroring my light, emotionally neutral tone exactly, he then said all the "right" things: "I had no idea. I am proud of you. It must have taken great courage."

Now came the tricky part—telling Frank and Max, my second and third sons, both of whom are married with kids. I couldn't seem to come up with a plan I felt comfortable with so I kept procrastinating. I knew telling them would raise some issues. Do they share this with their wives? If shared, will their wives be supportive or will their wives use it as an opportunity to point out how screwed up I was and use it as ammunition against me? How will they feel about my decision to take my bulimia public in order to help others battling the same adversary? These were more than palpable concerns; these were fears that at times paralyzed me.

I knew my sons could easily be appalled, disappointed, sickened and embarrassed by my revelations, but I also knew that my sons would always love me, never shun me. I was their mom and I had been a good one. I knew from them, after they digested the information, I would "get a pass" but I wasn't so sure a direct conversation with my married sons was the right way to broach the subject of my forty-six years of disordered eating.

I decided rather than a direct conversation with my boys, I would write them a letter—addressed to them at their respective offices. And just to keep everything on an even keel, I also sent the same letter to the other three boys at the same time even though they already knew. I decided to send it on the heels of the Jewish holidays of Rosh Hashanah and Yom Kippur.

Here's the first version of that letter:

> *Dear Harry, Frank, Max, Sam and Lou,*
> *This is the season of renewal and repair, thus this letter—to tell you about a demon I have battled for years.*
> *I have been bulimic since I was a sophomore at the University of Florida in 1966. What that means is practically every day of my life for the last forty-six years, I have binged and purged.*
> *In January 2012, I was in crisis. I knew I could not continue on this self-destructive path. Physical symptoms were beginning*

to manifest themselves and my fear of doing permanent harm to myself was growing. I entered a treatment center in Clearwater as an outpatient. The director was doubtful that I could successfully overcome my eating disorder without inpatient care. This was not an option as I was working full-time and at this point very few people knew. I was not comfortable in broadcasting this information. It was my personal secret and that was how I wanted it to stay.

I entered outpatient therapy in February, going three times a week for three hours, from four-fifteen to seven-fifteen p.m. I participated in group and individual therapy, art therapy and nutrition classes. I was closely monitored at meals. It was weird making the transition from a director at Jewish Federation to a patient at an eating disorders clinic, but I struggled through it.

In May 2012, the formal treatment was over and I left the safety of the institutional program. I continued with private therapy for a short time and then began on my own to practice the skills I had been taught to keep ED at bay.

I have now been bulimic-free for nineteen months. To complete my recovery, I started Weight Watchers in January 2013 and have lost twenty-two pounds through portion control and mindful eating.

I am writing you this in the hope that you will be proud of me for having the courage to face a personal demon. And I am writing to you in the hopes that if ever the time comes that you need to face a personal failing, you too will rise to the occasion, go for help and direct all your energies into healing.

Love,
Mom

I let Sam read the letter before I put it in an envelope and sent it off. "Whoa, Mom," he exclaimed. "WTMI. Way too much info." Here's his version:

Dear Boys,

I just want to let you know that like many of the female friends you have grown up with, I have had an eating disorder for most of my life. After forty-six years, it has been successfully treated. And I thought you would want to know.

Love,
Mom

"Sam," I implored, "that is way too short. It's ridiculous!"

We compromised. This is my new and more succinct version to the boys—the one I really did send:

September 6, 2013
Dear Harry, Frank, Max, Sam and Lou,
The Jewish New Year is a season of repair, atonement and renewal.

For forty-six years, I have battled a personal demon—I have been bulimic since I was a sophomore at the University of Florida. In January 2012, I was at a crossroads and knew I needed help. I entered a treatment program for my eating disorder.

In May 2012, my formal treatment was over and at this point, I have been free of my bulimia for nineteen months. I am telling you this because it is something that I feel very proud of overcoming and I am very thankful for this new beginning.

Love,
Mom

Why did I tell them?

I was proud of myself and wanted to share it with them.

I wanted them to have a positive role model when fighting their own demons.

I had already told some people, so I didn't want them not to know.

I had plans for taking my struggle and victory over ED public in some way—speaking, writing, volunteering, mentoring—at some yet-to-be-determined time and I didn't want them blindsided.

And there were the grandchildren—I wanted to raise the awareness that an eating disorder could have genetic roots.

I'm not sure how the band of brothers responded to each other upon the arrival of my note. I do know they checked in with each other to see if they had all received the same note. But Frank and Max each reacted in a manner that was predictable and in keeping with their natures.

Frank never responded, nor in any subsequent conversation we had did he allude to it. It didn't surprise me. Frank is the kindest, most accepting of my sons. He rarely gets mad at me, even if I am clearly in the wrong. He holds no grudges and is always there to lend a hand. Why the silence? The next time I visited him, I confirmed my hunch. Cornering him in the kitchen after his wife and kids had gone to bed, I asked him if he had gotten my note.

He knew immediately what note I was referring to. "Yep," he replied.

"Don't tell me," I bantered lightly. "Let me guess why you didn't respond. You didn't know what to say, right?"

He smiled tentatively and then hugged me hard.

Max is the son who puts things in silos. Max is the son who keeps his emotions close and goes out of his way, as a self-protective measure, to keep things on an even keel—to avoid complications, confrontations and the surfacing of any unresolved issues. I respect his boundaries. Shortly after receiving my note, Max texted me that he was glad to hear I had successfully overcome such a hard thing.

None of my sons reacted in a highly emotional way. There were no tears of joy. There were no toasts to mom's success. No congratulatory vases of roses arriving on my doorstep following my revelation. And I know why. For them, it was, and continues to be, an abstraction. They never watched me wolf down a gallon of ice cream at one sitting. They never heard the continual flushing of the commode nor smelled the lingering smell of vomit circulating in the air in the half bath. They never saw me emerge from the bathroom, with bloodshot eyes, flushed face and raw knuckles. They never hugged me and smelled the thrown-up food.

I am happy to have spared them that. They are my sons, not my friends. Not my guardian angels. Not my spouse, my siblings, nor my parents. Truth be told, if I had never intended to take my journey public, I would never have shared my saga of slaying ED with them in the first place.

Yearning for a Daughter, Accepting Sons

I admit it. I have always yearned for a daughter. And I didn't keep that yearning to myself.

Years ago, in numerous motivational speeches, I referred to myself as a daughterless mother. The same-sex intimacy, the shared female experience, the innate gender-based commonality were things that I missed. Meaningless chitchat. Hair care problems. Menstruation woes. Birthing. Nurturing. Aging. Personal affirmations I have created to define my female perspective. My sons had no interest—no point of relevancy.

I felt guilty complaining and yet the feeling of loss was there. The yearning for something illusive and not part of my everyday routine remained with me. Became part of who I was and how I defined myself. The feeling of wanting a daughter to pass on subliminally, subconsciously and naturally the experiences of being female stayed with me, set me apart. I feared my psychic connection to generations of female wisdom would abruptly be broken with me.

I comforted myself with the thought that I had eight nieces to love, cherish, nurture and spoil. And soon, one day perhaps, a granddaughter of my own with whom I could share my stories—for whom I could serve as a mile marker against which she will measure her own travels. Perhaps the bond to female offspring was still to be determined.

Following is a column I wrote about my unfulfilled wish for female offspring.

I'm grateful. I'm content. I'm thankful for my lot. Most of the time.

Over the years, I have always longed for a daughter. Sometimes more. Sometimes less. But always there was a small ache in my heart—an unfulfilled yearning just beyond my grasp.

When my friends were giving birth to little baby girls, I watched with envy as they fiddled with clip-on bows for hairless little heads. I was tripping over toy trucks.

When my friends were raising four-year-old little girls, I watched with envy as they dressed them in white tights and dresses with smocking and painted their finger nails bright red. I was tripping over toy trucks.

And over the years, as these same little girls blossomed into young women who challenged their mother's every word, angrily slammed doors in their mother's faces and screamed "I hate you" more than once, I still watched with envy. I knew someday they would be back.

As a mother of sons, I've taken to carefully observing girls and their mothers. During Rosh Hashanah services at temple, I was seated in back of a family with three girls and I was treated to a rich array of action.

I watched how the oldest sister patiently spoke to the youngest one, who was sitting on her mother's lap. I didn't once in the hour and one half observe them utter the words butthead, suck or shut up. They didn't push, shove, kick or bite.

Now I assume they must do their share of whining, crying, complaining and bitching at home, but they didn't that day at services. They looked at their mother lovingly, touched her frequently and listened intently to her comments and remarks.

The two older girls had beautifully manicured nails, just like their mother, and the youngest girl wore her purse slung jauntily across her chest, just like her mom.

That night my husband and I took a walk.

"I'm grateful. I'm content. I'm thankful for my lot," I started telling my husband, as we rounded the first bend.

190

"Okay, what's the matter?" he asked automatically.

"Well, while I have eight beautiful nieces and high hopes of someday having prolific daughters-in-law who give birth to lots of little girls, I don't have a daughter," I responded.

"And it makes me sad," I added.

"Somehow, having always had little ones around, albeit little male ones, somehow the void never seemed quite as large as it does now. But when I kissed Louie goodnight last night, instead of being kissed right back, I got, 'Mom, that's disgusting.'

"When I reminded him that just two weeks ago when he fell off his bike and roughly skinned both his knees, my kisses and hugs were okay, he replied, 'That was then, this is now.' And rolled over, closed his eyes and went to sleep. And that's when I knew I was in trouble," I concluded.

"And you'll never lose your boys," I further lamented. "They'll always be your sons but I'll be replaced by girlfriends, lovers and wives. No one will want me!" I wailed.

We walked in silence for awhile after my outburst.

"What will make you happy?" my husband gently probed.

"Just one more," I said.

"But it could be a boy, you know," my husband reminded me ever so firmly.

"That wouldn't be so bad, either," I shot back. Visions of delicious chubby thighs and warm velvety necks flashed through my mind.

We were almost home. It was late and I was getting tired. Thoughts of taking a very hot shower and then crawling into clean, cool sheets assaulted my senses. Thoughts of changing dirty diapers and comforting a teething, cranky baby didn't seem so inviting.

I wondered if Louie had finished sorting his baseball cards; if Sam had practiced his spelling words; and if Max was still on the phone. Suddenly I couldn't wait to get home.

"Come on," I good-naturedly challenged my husband, "I'll race you back."

Letting go of ED helped me shed outmoded beliefs, habits and mind frames I had steadfastly embraced and clung to. Letting go of ED also helped me unharness my yearnings for female offspring.

I am now fully accepting of the fact that my sons won't and can't and don't choose to behave as daughters. I am now *almost* fully accepting of the fact that I am not, nor will I ever be, privy to the minutiae of their days, nor will I ever completely understand the intensely emotional interest they exhibit towards the Cincinnati Reds and The Ohio State University Buckeyes.

However, I have gently—and at times not so gently—finally pried myself loose from the many gender-based expectations I had for them. I have stopped making myself miserable trying to make my sons behave like daughters—measuring their love by how much they call, text, share their days, send cards, and post loving accolades to me as their mother on Facebook, etc. I have always loved and adored my five boys, but never fully appreciated them as males because I was so blinded by my lack of a female child. How foolish I was.

Now that I have stopped trying to make them into something they are not—which is daughters—I am fully able to embrace and appreciate the awesome men my sons have become. They are busy, productive and responsible men who love their mother even though days can pass without a touch-base moment. It was a big breakthrough for me.

Fortunately, I have been blessed with three warm, caring, and understanding daughters-in-law—who graciously accept me with all my imperfections. And ironically, though I never did get my longed-for daughter, I am blessed with three healthy, fully-functioning, beautiful granddaughters. My female connection. My girly legacy. My flesh-and-blood generational link of Y chromosomes—all who seem to share my need to connect, talk, share and communicate on a regular basis.

Post-Treatment Behavior: Baking

I found that after treatment, I no longer craved ice cream of any kind or flavor. Maybe I did deep down, for ice cream was always my go-to food when bingeing—simply because it was so easy to throw up. Like a tsunami, it carried along with it whatever was in its path. But as the months passed, it never reappeared on my favorite foods list.

For a while I was on a baking kick. Looking back it probably had little to do with pleasing my husband by baking tempting goodies so he could maintain his weight (he was one of those disgusting people who had to make a concerted effort to keep from losing pounds!). I think returning to baking was about getting in touch with and embracing my hunger for life in general—without the weighty harness of bulimia. Physical hunger was one of the hungers I was re-acquainting myself with. Going back to working with my hands and making something edible of worth and value from "nothing" was a way of also satisfying my hunger for creating.

Baking also tested my newly emerging resolve. There were two dangerous intersections to transverse. The first was after mixing all the ingredients together, right before pouring the batter into loaf pans. Could I resist spooning the rich and creamy batter into my mouth? Could I resist licking the bowl and the mixer blades (after removing them, that is!)? The next dangerous intersection was immediately after the baked goodie emerged from the oven and was cooling on the wire rack. Could I resist the smell of the vanilla flavoring wafting through the kitchen? Could I limit myself to just one slice at a time?

The days roll by. I rotate my baking routine: zucchini bread, banana bread, pumpkin bread or carrot cake. But my after-baking behavior remains the same. After all the ingredients are measured out, mixed and poured into loaf pans, I quickly fill the ceramic mixing bowl with soapy water and submerge the mixing blades immediately into that same soapy mess. Only then do I allow myself to lick the wooden spoon and slide my tongue over the floppy spatula still dripping with batter.

My glass pedestal cake holder displays my home-baked goods. The slices disappear quickly—but not by me. I am able to eat a slice a day, training myself to leisurely chew, mindfully taste and slowly savor the richness of the slice.

Having passed that "test," I lose interest in baking daily. Sorry, Steven.

Lunch With a Friend

At least once a week, I lunch with a friend.

We avoid small talk and gossip—most of the time.

We usually talk baby boomer substance—a mix of wry humor, lighthearted banter and serious shit.

We brainstorm how to overcome the challenges of difficult relatives.

We ponder how to remain close to our adult offspring without smothering them. How to be caretakers to our aging parents without smothering ourselves.

We joke about our thinning hair on the crown of our heads.

We explore how to stop our teeth from further yellowing.

And of course, we discuss men—the ones in our lives, the ones who used to be in our lives, and for some of us (not me) those men we are hoping to come along and be part of our lives.

Ordering food was always a problem for me.

I used to search out the low-calorie, low-fat menu items.

I shunned the sweet potato fries, the chicken pot pie, the Reuben sandwich, all of which I secretly craved.

Now I order what I am in the mood for and I enjoy the indulgence, keeping in mind portion control.

My friends and I have yet to solve the mysteries of the universe, nor halt the indignities of age, or fully tame our little corner of the planet.

But, I'm not getting fat in the process and I'm enjoying and savoring both the food and the friend.

This Was My Day

Someone cuts me off in traffic? Someone puts me on hold too long? I swallow my anger.

Mad at myself for eating three helpings of pasta at dinner? I finish the day with a pint of ice cream.

Two friends I introduced to each other leave me out of their lunches? I stifle my hurt feelings.

My son calls to tell me his plans for the weekend—most of which revolve around his wife's family? I push down my envy.

When my sons plan parties to celebrate their milestone birthdays—and leave my husband and me off the guest list? I squash my disappointment.

When I change my plans so that I can drive a friend to the airport, I push aside my irritation at her tepid "thank you."

I punish myself for my ugly, not perfect body.

I hang onto past hurts.

I focus on what wounds my feelings—what makes me sad—what aggravates me.

And I find plenty to stew about:

- Kids don't call enough—the minutiae of their lives remains a mystery.
- Emails to friends who have moved away go unanswered.
- My maj group ladies talk incessantly about outings to the zoo, the hamburger shack, the baseball games with the in-town grandchildren, not realizing how much long-distance grandparenting sucks.
- Couples glorify their trips to Europe—reliving in minute detail the trains, the sights, the smells the shopping. My husband and I have never been.

- Neighbors show off their new car, their newest designer hand bag, their newly renovated swimming pool. None of which my pocketbook can accommodate.

What happens?
- Feelings of deprivation lead me to faulty feelings of hunger.
- Eating only temporarily assuages the pain.
- Eating only temporarily provides a refuge from the existential emptiness.

I'm not really yearning for food, I realize, but for inclusion, consistent connection, relevancy, engagement.

This Is Going to Be My Day

When I start feeling envious that my friends enjoy unlimited access to their grandchildren, I am going to remind myself that soon I will be seeing mine.

And because the time is limited, the time I spend with them on the floor building castles out of wooden blocks is all the sweeter.

I am embracing the emptiness.

Filling it up with enjoyable activities:
- Yin yoga
- Reading
- Knitting
- Walking
- Lunching
- Writing
- Pondering, creating and exploring
- Beckoning new opportunities to appear
- Receptively embracing them when they do
- If I can't have what I want, I will want what I have.

When I begin wishing that my kids needed me more, I will remind myself that independent offspring is a badge of good parenting which frees up my time—to register for the collage class down the street, to pick up the lost art of bike riding, to master Middle Eastern cooking.

When spending another birthday away from my family, I will plan a party with newfound friends to go kayaking on the river instead of choosing to sit cross-legged at home on my family room couch, crying.

When I stick to my plan of taking two yoga classes a week for three months, I will celebrate the milestone by purchasing a new yoga mat. Not lament my inability to still execute Downward Dog without tipping over.

When I receive monogrammed note pads in the mail from my mom, decked out with my name in bold red letters, I will use them for grocery lists and random thoughts, rather than stashing them in the junk drawer to be saved for a special time.

I am beginning to prize my body—in spite of jiggly kneecaps and a sagging tush.

I am starting to like the length of my hair, appreciating its continued thickness and luster.

I pay silent accolades to my oily skin that resists wrinkling.

I am thankful for inheriting the dimple in my chin from my paternal grandmother—although the sagging around it still irks.

I buy a full-length mirror for my bedroom wall.

And I start studying myself.

I take renewed interest in mixing and matching the varied pieces of my eclectic wardrobe—the flowing scarves, the ethnic necklaces, the funky hats.

I buy a vintage frame, outfitted with interior netting, to showcase my dangly earrings and every morning I pick out a different pair to wear.

I listen to the compliments I get—rather than brusquely, as in the past, shunting them aside as irrelevant. Or empty flattery.

I am beginning to look for ways to keep myself healthy and fit.

I go for full body scans to check out suspicious skin tags and moles.

I get my hearing checked and my teeth cleaned twice yearly.

I do physical therapy for a bum shoulder.

I get regularly scheduled massages to relieve the tension buildup in my neck and shoulders.

Pap smears, bone density tests, mammograms—no longer just on my to-do list, but now posted on my daily calendar.

I read the comics.

I go to the beach—alternating my route for brain health.

I watch Dr. Oz.

When I find from his show that cherries are good for reducing inflammation in the body, I try to eat some every day.

I like me.

This Is My Day

I now have a different reaction to unreturned emails and phone calls, delayed responses and indifferent reactions. I don't take them as a personal affront to me; rather, I tell myself it's that person's situation that is the cause of their actions, not mine.

I invite a couple over two times for Sunday brunch, but never get a return invitation. The next time I plan a brunch, I skip them and invite the friendly couple from my yoga class instead.

I re-work my reaction to a close friend's somewhat direct, uncensored feedback on my table manners and bohemian wardrobe choices. I no longer view her comments as an attack, but as helpful hints—guideposts—imparting to me valuable feedback on how I can improve myself.

And when I don't get what I need? I ask.

Realizing that most of my maj group helps the hostess clean up before leaving, I no longer sulk silently that no one ever helps me. Could it be that when help is offered, I protest mightily? Now I stifle my protests and graciously welcome the help in closing down the card table and throwing the maj tiles back in the carrying case.

Before, I would swallow my irritation when a longtime friend from college days would extol the virtues of her dead husband when I knew the marriage was mostly a sham. Now I encourage her to tell me about some of her fond memories. I am amazed at the information imparted. How could I not know he was an expert carpenter who built her anything she asked? How did I not know he brought her breakfast in bed every morning when she was incapacitated with a broken ankle?

When I make a special effort to bake carrot cake and banana bread for my husband and he is not as overjoyed or appreciative of my efforts as I had hoped he would be, I don't go into a sulking funk. Instead, I hug him hard and whisper in his ear that it's my way of showing him how important he is to me.

I've actually started reading the self-help books I have accumulated over the years—instead of just admiring how nice they look on my white wicker bookshelves in the guest room.

Driving a friend to the airport? I no longer stew about the outlay of time, but seize the opportunity to learn more about her South African roots.

Years ago when I assumed the full care of my elderly, childless aunt, I was astounded by the inner resources she employed to keep her fears engendered by her physical frailty in check. When she no longer felt safe in her room in the nursing home, she and her friend stationed themselves in close proximity to the nurse's desk—not only did they get to see the floor action, but were in range of immediate help if needed.

I wondered if I would be so adaptable.

One morning, right before my youngest son's Bar Mitzvah, all my kids were sitting around the kitchen table pouring varying obscene amounts of pancake syrup on their stacks. My aunt was still very much on my mind.

"Hey, guys," I lightly questioned, "when I am old and feeble, which one of you will come to the nursing home and pluck my chin hairs?"

Dead silence ensued.

And then they all seemed to answer at once. "Mom," they uttered with reassurance, "don't worry. We will take turns paying someone to do it."

It was not the response I was seeking.

At first I was horrified. Vastly disappointed. Because what I was really asking, I later realized, was who will love me? Who will visit me? Who will pay attention to me and protect me when I am old and needy?

Their answer haunted me for years. Paying someone? Over time, I was able to reframe my attitude toward their spontaneous answer—to re-frame it in a way that provided me reassurance that my sons did indeed love me and would take care of me.

Here's my spin on their paying someone to pluck my chin hairs:
- They recognize my need.
- They exhibit optimism in their ability to provide for me.
- They demonstrate siblings working in unison.
- They act in response to my request.

So what happens now when I find myself not liking a situation? Not liking the way someone else responds to a situation?

I find a new angle. I crop. I edit. I re-frame and re-work.

Worry over my elderly mom eating out by herself? I am thankful she is still driving.

Obsessing why heads don't turn when I walk into a restaurant? I am thankful I can still strut my stuff in four-inch heels without breaking my shinbones.

Angry over going up a size in my jeans? Ah, now I take a breath without fear of hyperventilating and passing out cold.

I'm lowering my impossibly high expectations for myself and for others.

I am breaking out of the prison of my own making.

And letting the bad stuff go.

I'm seeking the positive.

Finding it.

Reveling in it.

Prizing it.

While weaving my own tale and spinning my own cocoon.

White Space

I am a time-efficiency crazy person.

My aim is to pack everything I can into every moment. That's why Fitbit is so satisfying a way to get in my exercise. It's a device that automatically counts the number of my steps each day. It's portable—I clip it onto my underpants and check the Fitbit app on my iPhone periodically during the day to monitor my progress.

I continue to find unique ways to increase the number of steps I take each day—again, without wasting time.

Elevators work wonders for increasing my steps—especially slow, empty ones. I rigorously march in place as the floor numbers fly by. Standing in lines—aha, that's no longer irritating at all. I rigorously march in place there too. Of course, those in line closest to me look at me with concern and often a tad of apprehension. One kind lady asked if I was in need of a toilet. Another inquired if I was in an ardent hurry. Lines at Starbucks at any airport during peak holiday times are no longer a major irritant, but a sure-fire way of accumulating steps.

Then there's unpacking—especially when I leave my fully-loaded suitcases downstairs and carry up piles of clothes continuously until the suitcase is bare.

My goal is 18,000 steps a day—and believe it or not, I usually reach it.

If I come up a few thousand steps short as midnight approaches, I walk in a circle around the couch facing the TV and listen as I walk.

Though I adhere to this crazy schedule, I find I am no longer stressed nor exhausted. Actually, I am more relaxed and productive.

Weird. How can this be?

Dan Blank, who helps writers share their stories and connect with readers, is my guru. So when a recent blog post of his defined the concept of "White Space" as necessary to a writer's well-being and productivity, I was enthralled.

As Dan says, "Sleep matters. Seriously. Unscheduled time matters. Time with family or loved ones matters. Alone time matters... it's where bad habits are negated and where we honor the need for the space in between other things in our lives." He refers to this time as "White Space."

I was horrified to learn that as a grown man he takes a nap every afternoon. "What a waste," I scoff judgmentally to myself. "A half-hour nap is worth 3,000 steps around the couch!"

I learn a lot from reading Dan's readers' comments:

What does White Space do?

- Clears the brain
- Prompts viewing a situation from a new angle
- Allows the brain to wander, naturally stimulating the imagination
- Helps us absorb our experiences and understand the world around us
- Provides balance between productivity and refueling our energy banks
- Refreshes us
- Purges mind fog
- Cuts down on quantitative measurement of our performance

How do we get white space?

- Yoga
- Napping
- Mindful breathing
- Hobbies
- Online game playing
- Reading the comics
- Goofing off
- Journaling
- Dancing
- Lighting a scented candle

- Puttering with plants
- Sketching

With a jolt, I realize walking throughout my day to reach a set number of steps provides me with frequent mini-breaks. It is time that chills me out while wholly rejuvenating my creative juices. It's my own personalized "White Space."

"White Space" can be anything you want it to be. The most important thing is knowing what works for you and doing it.

Ah. Nirvana.

Entertaining

I decide to host a Chanukah lunch for my book group.

I plan the menu. I set the table with my mom's good bone china, my aunt's sterling silver cutlery and my grandmother's antique teacups. I fry potato latkes from scratch and buy rich butter cookies in the shape of dreydels from a nearby upscale bakery.

The lunch is a roaring success.

When the guests depart, I am tired and I am alone. The silence is soothing after the tumultuous chatter. Turning on classical music, I hum contentedly to myself as I begin leisurely cleaning up. I savor the comments I received from my friends about the warmth of my home and the effort I expended. I clear the dishes from the dining room table. I pile the linens in a corner for future washing. I soap off the good china and silver. I pick at the loose pieces of potato pancakes and eat two of the butter cookies before I wrap up the leftovers, which are destined for one of my sons who lives nearby.

It's not until I go to bed that night that I realize fully the sea change that has occurred.

Entertaining as a bulimic was agonizing. All the foods I normally avoided storing in the house were taking up temporary residence on my counters. Keeping me unfocused and agitated.

I didn't join in the good-natured banter with my friends. I didn't laugh at my husband's jokes. I didn't listen avidly to a colleague's travel vignette. All my concentration was centered on how I could convince my husband to let me clean up by myself when the party was over. Why? So all those forbidden leftover goodies would be mine. Why? So I could shovel the remaining potato puffs and chocolate éclairs into my mouth as fast as I could. Why? So I could, minutes later, violently and relentlessly expel it all into the toilet.

This time, I basked in the high points of the party—seeing my friends seated around my dining room table, chatting and laughing. I took pleasure from using the accoutrements I have been lucky enough to inherit. I drew happiness from decorating the house with Chanukah decorations my grown children had made in grade school. I savored the compliments from well-meaning friends. I cherished the warm and affectionate hugs and cheek kisses as they said good-bye.

Entertaining was no longer a demanding exercise laced with subterfuge and distraction. I'm not exactly sure when the sea change took place, but I am very thankful it did.

Vulnerability

Question: What scared me most about my bulimia?

Answer: Continuing on the same path I was going, thus causing irreparable damage to my body. Exposing myself to the world as bulimic, thus confirming I was less than perfect.

How ironic that when I dared unmask my vulnerability and asked people close to me to write something about my bulimia—and I purposely kept my request shrouded in vagueness—their overriding reactions were centered on how proud they were of me for confronting my addiction and moving forward to help others by sharing my journey.

Researcher and author Bréne Brown, in her TED Talk on "The Power of Vulnerability" notes, "It appears that vulnerability is the birthplace of joy, creativity, longing and love."

It certainly holds true in my case.

Jean's Response

I've known Iris for a long time, but never really "knew" her until my husband and I moved to Tampa in 2012. When we were both living in Cincinnati, we traveled in the same circle, but never got to know each other really well. When I called her after we moved south, we talked for a long time, as if we had been friends forever. We were both writers, working moms, creative types trying out new approaches to our craft. It was as if we had been friends forever, confidantes, BFFs. If we had been thirteen, we would have slept over at each other's houses many times.

Iris was (and is) just beautiful: high cheekbones, smooth skin, huge eyes, long lashes, bow lips, with an enviable figure. Her energy and flair lit her up. She was so open about her hopes and dreams: what she wanted for her children, her husband, and herself. She wanted to help people, hoped to be able to do that through her writing. She would send me something she had worked on, and I was always impressed by her clarity and willingness to open up.

One hot Florida day she and I were swimming in my pool when she said she wanted to tell me something personal. I couldn't imagine what she was going to say—I hoped it wasn't anything troubling about her family. She tread water for a minute and then came out with it. "I've been bulimic for many years and no one knows it." I certainly had no idea. Bulimic? I thought this was something that affected teenage girls; Iris, like me, was in her sixties. Can you acquire bulimia in your sixties? What would make you want to binge and purge at our age? I had eaten several meals with Iris and I didn't remember her stuffing herself and then running to the bathroom. I had no idea and the look on my face when she told me must have betrayed my shock and horror.

Iris confessed all, from the beginnings to her recovery. I had known none of this. True, we had only been real friends for a short time, but we had become so close. It didn't seem possible. As she talked, though, I couldn't help but admire her even more. She had confessed all to her husband Steven and to her five sons. She had sought treatment on her own, and managed to work at recovery while keeping up her busy schedule of work, writing, and grandmothering. This strength of hers would be called upon and demonstrated over and over a couple of years hence when she helped Steven through a long and debilitating illness.

Iris told me that she wanted to write something about how bulimia affected baby boomers. I didn't know that anything so terrible affected baby boomers; I thought that our thinning hair, dry skin, and sagging breasts were our cross to bear. Iris assured me that bulimia was more universal in women our age than I could ever know. She would write a book about her recovery in order to help women our age take the steps to their own healing.

And so she has done it. To those who know her, know her determination, her compassion, and her willingness to share her life, this will come as no surprise.

Gloria's Reaction

Secrets are powerful. When you choose to share a personal and precious one, you are revealing a part of yourself that is vulnerable. You are taking a chance that you might be met with shock, disdain, incredibility or misunderstanding. We are all a lot more than how we appear on the outside. And we never know how we are seen by others. Some of us are better at "putting on a face" than others.

At first, I was shocked by your admission yet impressed by how you were able to keep it a secret. I had no idea at all. But I never felt that you were dishonest—that you did not share it with me. It was yours to own. I think of your secret as painful and private, not shameful. I just don't. Shame can only be a personal issue, not a word of judgment. That is just not a friend's job.

I am so proud of your facing the challenge of overcoming your disorder and bravely conquering it.

I am not in any way surprised by your honesty, strength, sense of humor and great courage. I have been privileged to share many of my life celebrations and struggles with you. You have lifted me up, took hold of me and helped me to replace anger and fear with optimism and confidence. When you call it "my shameful little secret," I feel like that is not fair. It is yours. It was a secret, but shameful? Not at all.

You will certainly help others who may be fighting this demon or other demons that seem insurmountable. I am so lucky to have been part of this process.

Touching Tawny

Tawny and I met each other in first grade, in Mrs. Norcross's room, in Bond Hill School in Cincinnati, Ohio in 1953.

We shared something in common—our size. It would be a bond that kept us tied together for our entire lives. But I am getting ahead of myself.

She was a big kid for her age, with a full face surrounded by thick, brown braids. I too was a big kid for my age, with a full face, surrounded by a thick, brown ponytail.

Ironically, almost from the moment Tawny and I met, we nicknamed each other Sugar, a moniker we still use today—though now the phrase is heavy with irony. We forged an unsinkable bond—and maybe our subconscious knew what we didn't: we were bound by more than just friendship. We were bound by cravings for sugar and all that sugar represented. We each had found a kindred soul.

I remember doing sleepovers at her house. It was a Tudor style two-story, with leaded glass windows that let in little natural light, closed bedroom doors, and an unused living room and dining room. Her parents had divorced, and her father had remarried. She learned at an early age that she had to take care of herself.

My house was different. The rooms were fully utilized, basked in light, filled with me and my siblings' activities. I had a hands-on mother who worried that if I slept out too much I would get dissipated, who made sure I ate healthy food, drank plenty of milk and never skipped breakfast. I learned early on that I didn't have to take care of myself because that was my mom's job.

I don't remember much about our junior high years but I know I envied Tawny's ability to twirl a baton, though I happily applauded her victory when she made majorette. I tried out for cheerleading, but I was too clumsy.

Tawny had a steady boyfriend, dyed her hair red, and instituted a self-imposed study schedule.

I had a steady boyfriend, but kept my hair brown or my mom would have killed me. I studied hard too.

We spent our freshman year together at the University of Cincinnati. She had a green VW Bug that we tooled around in, listening to the Beatles' song "Yesterday" and lamenting about our senior year in high school being way more fun than freshman year at university. When we drove on the highway and the wind was high, the whole car shook. We thought it was hilarious.

Winter quarter, both Tawny and I moved into the dorm for ten weeks and shared a room. Like our dorm mates, we ordered in pizza at eleven p.m. Like my dorm mates, my weight ballooned. Tawny's didn't. I wondered why.

Though I didn't know it at the time, once again Tawny had found a clever, neat way to "take care of herself" in perilous waters. She had ED.

School proved too depressing because my high school boyfriend and I had broken up and he was already dating someone new—a blonde from Cleveland who lived on the floor above me. I begged my parents to let me transfer. At the beginning of my sophomore year, I started at the University of Florida. By the time I finished my first quarter in Gainesville, I had found a replacement for my mom—a lifelong companion called ED.

In our mid-twenties, Tawny and I both went through painful divorces, but there our paths diverged. Somehow, during her healing, she was once again able to take care of herself. After about fifteen years, she shed the bulimia—not sure how—and began eating healthily, exercising regularly and doing good things for herself.

I too was eating healthy, exercising regularly and doing good things for myself. Until nine p.m. every night, when ED visited and wrecked it all.

I lost touch with Tawny for many years. Intermittently, we would connect by phone or letter or even a quick lunch or walk, but seeing her was painful. It reminded me of how weak I was and how if I just perhaps tried a little harder, I could oust ED from my life too.

So I kept my distance.

I would like to say that when I made the decision to kick ED out permanently, I reached out to my old friend Tawny. She had implored me long ago to call her when I felt a binge coming on—said it was the only way she was able to kick the habit—by reaching out to someone when she sensed ED's presence. For some reason, I just couldn't do it.

Until years later, when I had been bulimic-free for many months. I then made the call to reconnect us and suggested lunch. An innocent bystander would describe us as two attractive, trim, middle-aged women vigorously enjoying each other's company. And they would be right. We talked of many things. I told her of my progress. I could sense that she felt sad that she could not have been of more help. I felt sad too.

Tawny and I are in the throes of planning a trip to Europe—London and Paris—for ten days this summer. She is a seasoned traveler. I am not. But she has promised to show me the ropes, lead the way. This time I am accepting her offer of help and guidance.

We all need a little "Sugar" in our lives.

WTF

Anger management is an important element in dealing with beating an eating disorder. Duh.

What I have learned over the last three years is that blowing your top is not such a bad thing. Feels pretty damn good, actually.

It's not surprising that a study conducted by Sandra Thomas, a professor at the University of Tennessee, found that older women who expressed their anger—albeit in healthier ways than blowing their stacks—had lower levels of the inflammatory markers linked to cardiovascular disease. What a smart lady that one is.

I figure I must be, by now, the healthiest chick on the planet. Since beating ED, my use of the F-word has soared. It is my go-to adjective and verb of choice. Used vociferously. Uttered with great gusto.

And my most favorite expression—to the displeasure of most of my family—has become WTF.

Thank you *AARP* magazine for providing me with such unabashed reinforcement that indeed I am on the right path to a sustainable recovery and continued physical robustness.

Hot damn.

To Tell or Not to Tell My Mom

Telling my mom about my bulimia?
Ha ha.
That's another matter entirely.
She is a widow.

She is ninety years old.
She is hard of hearing.
She lives by herself.
She is lonely, though surrounded by lifelong friends.
She lives comfortably within her means, but misses my dad.
I am her firstborn "golden" child.
Harnessed with the moniker of the one who "keeps it all together."
How can I burst that bubble?
Yet how can I not pursue my own path?
Maybe she will get just a tad senile in the next couple of months?
Becoming less aware of her surroundings?
Getting me off the hook?
Right. Dream on.
She remembers the things I forget.
She balances her checkbook to the penny.
She follows the local news with a passion.
She just starred in a highly acclaimed TV commercial to save a
    local Cincinnati landmark.
She does word puzzles every day.
She still has a keen sense of direction.
She checks her email hourly.
And Googles for answers.
"Fat" chance she won't notice I publish a book on bulimia.

August 18, 2015

Wow, what a revelation I had today.

Picture this: for months I had been telling my husband that I was not angry at him for not taking a more active role in helping me break my binge/purge cycle of disordered eating. Whenever he would broach any sentiments bordering on regret, I would quickly and routinely short-circuit the conversation and emphatically state that was how I had wanted it. It had been my battle and I had not wanted him involved.

And yet, as the months passed and work in earnest began on my editing of this book, I noticed—and so did he—that more often than not, I replied to him in a very snippy tone, regardless of the topic of conversation. Where was this bitchiness coming from? Paradoxically, this was months after his very invasive back surgeries and his near-brush with death due to an infection that literally ate his vertebrae. And after I played a relentless and essential role in his rebound, rehabilitation and recovery.

I couldn't figure out my behavior. Was it a very delayed reaction? But to what? All I could decipher was that my irritation and short-tempered attitude toward him seemed to intensify as out routine returned to normal following his extended hospital stays and recuperation.

I had asked him to write something for this book because I felt strongly that without his input and observations, the full story would not be told. We both agreed he needed to do a little soul-searching concerning his lack of a role in my return to good health. And yet, when he deftly read aloud to me his first draft, fury descended on me. His words were both trite and vacuous. Crestfallen, I tearfully fled his presence.

Distressed by my reaction, he decided to call a therapist we had both seen together in the past when beset with some marital issues we needed to work through. Alas, the therapist would be gone until August, so my husband had about eight weeks to figure out some things. Why was he paralyzed by inaction when confronted with my bulimia? Why did he passively sit back and do nothing to further his understanding of my disordered eating? Why did he allow my protestations to override his good sense?

And I really did believe—up until about an hour ago—that I bore him no ill will, harbored no anger regarding his passivity around my bulimia. Why? Because I had emphatically instructed him "to butt out."

We had just returned from a three-week journey to see both our mothers in Ohio and our three sons, two daughters-in-law and five

212

grandchildren in the New York area. We were both hanging up clothes in our closet and discussing what calls we had to make now that we were home.

"You know," I suddenly burst out, "I think I am really angry with you about your not stepping up to the plate for me all the years you knew I was bulimic.

"A lot of memories came tumbling out while we were in Cincinnati," I continued. "And I found myself thinking quite a bit about your behavior during the six months your dad battled pancreatic cancer.

"You certainly stepped up to the plate when your dad got sick. You certainly pulled out all the stops for him, even to the point of disregarding your own health problems at the time. Health problems," I bitterly reminded him, "that plague you to this day and have impacted and altered our lives dramatically."

"Iris," he shot back, "there was no one else to do it for him."

Dead silence.

As I digested this kernel of new information, blind fury swirled around me, descending like a shroud, encapsulating my body.

"Really?" I snapped back icily.

"Really?" I repeatedly screamed. "Really? Really? Really?"

I collapsed in a sobbing, hysterical heap on the closet floor.

My husband was more than frightened by my outburst. He was totally taken aback by my rage—my visceral reaction to his statement.

"Let me get this straight," I hurled at him with unbridled fury. "You have three other siblings, but you were the only one who could do it? You were the only one who could advocate for him on his behalf?"

"Yes," he said in a matter of fact tone. "Because I was the only son."

His words hung in the air.

A strange icy calm slipped over me. I stopped my sobbing. I wrapped my arms around myself. I started to sway and rock back and forth. Back and forth. Back and forth.

He bent down toward my crumpled figure. "Are you okay?" he pried gently.

"Okay?" I screamed. "Do you even know what you just said?"

He stared back at me with a bewildered look and furrowed brow.

"Let me get this straight," I shot back through clenched teeth. "Let me get this straight. There were five of you—you and your three sisters and your mom—yet you still feel that you were the one who had to relentlessly and ceaselessly be there for your father?

"Who in the fuck was supposed to be there for me?" I demanded. "Who in the fuck was supposed to be there for me when I was sick? I only had one husband."

He was shocked by my anger. And my judgment. But I wasn't. It had been simmering for months. In the form of minor annoyance. Raw irritation. Rude impatience.

I struggled to my feet, walked out of the closet, slammed the door and let the rage I had been holding in for months spill out.

What was wrong with me?

What was wrong with him?

What was wrong with us?

My puzzlement continued, as did my anger. We both needed to find out why he dropped the ball and why I had been so willing to fight this battle alone.

Steven's Story (In His Own Words)

This is Iris's memoir, where she writes about moments and events concerning her bulimia.

What was private is now public. And when it comes to my role, or lack of one, concerning her bulimia, it is right on the mark. Especially after her outburst of rage, my lack of action was something I had to address.

I have had the opportunity of reading Iris's memoir numerous times and each reading when it addresses my role, the words are consistent. They do not change because they are true and accurate.

I have danced the dance of life with Iris for more than forty years, thus I could eagerly discuss the intensity, intimacy and caring of our marriage. That too would be honest, but just gingerbread to my lack of presence in her struggle with her eating disorder.

In fact, I cannot even remember when or even the circumstances under which she confessed to me that she was bulimic. However, since that time, it has always been the elephant in our relationship.

I do remember that she was adamant that I not intervene or interfere in any way to try to help her, and if I did, she said it would jeopardize our marriage. Boy did I comply. And it was my inaction and failure to intervene which has caused the greatest angst in my life, bar none, so far.

I viewed myself as Iris's knight in shining armor, but in actuality, I was a tarnished shadow of myself. She is my soul mate, the love of my life, the one whom I vowed to take care of in both sickness and in health. But I did nothing to help her fight her demon.

The question that haunts me is why I was so nonplussed. She asked me for nothing and that is what she received. It would be a cop-out to say that I respected her request. No! I believed in retrospect she was reaching out to me in a convoluted way for help and I wasn't there in any fashion or form. This is in deep contrast to my nature of being proactive toward and protective of Iris. Yet, I did nothing but pay lip service to her struggle.

I was a ghost. I rarely brought up the subject of her bulimia. Days, weeks, years would pass, but I was silent. If I addressed it at all, I would ask, "How are you doing?," which was the code phrase for, "Are you still vomiting?" But we never discussed the proverbial elephant's footprints in our living room. The footprints conveyed the unspoken.

Was I truly afraid that my participation would jeopardize our marriage? Perhaps, but even so, wasn't her health and welfare more important than what could have been simply a veiled threat? Why didn't I research the disease itself? Could I have spoken to health professionals to get a better perspective and understanding of what she was going through? I certainly knew bulimia nervosa was a serious, potentially life-threatening eating disorder, but I went no further to educate myself on its inherent perils and available treatment options.

Interestingly, re-reading Iris's memoir and articulating my shame has been therapeutic and cathartic. It has allowed me to help forgive myself in my overall failure to be an effective partner and advocate. It's my personal mea culpa.

I still do not have all the answers to the questions that have manifested, albeit I certainly know more about her relationship with ED and the signs to look for in the disease.

However, even to this day, in over five years into her remission, we do not really discuss her bulimia. Will the cycle repeat itself? I am certainly conscious of this possibility. Not as a policeman, but as her lover of more than forty years.

I chose not to go through extensive therapy to try to find out the cause or causes of my inability to react to Iris's bulimia in a productive and helpful manner. There has been no formal regurgitation of my inadequate response to Iris's disordered eating patterns. And it is a burden laced with regret and guilt that I bear to this day.

Are there other wounds I carry which impacted my failure to act? Maybe. Time does not heal all wounds, but I am dropping off the backpack of my guilt and lightening my load. Some things and some situations in life are never really fully resolved. Compromise and acceptance allow Iris and me to walk into the sunset together—imperfectly joined, but still perfectly matched.

And yes, I will always picture her in her brown skirt with the white polka dots—whether it is too tight, fitting snugly or hanging loosely. To me it does not matter. It is and has always has been her smile and her substance, not her size, that captured my heart that long ago night in 1975 when we re-met at our tenth high school reunion.

Anonymity

The definition of anonymity, according to *Webster's Encyclopedic Unabridged Dictionary of the English Language*, is "without any name acknowledgement."

How I longed to publish my book anonymously—without any trace of my name. For long hours on lazy afternoons when my writing pace become mired in fatigue, pen names danced in my head. My favorite soon became Telsey Diamond. It was a combination of my paternal grandmother's maiden name and my maternal grandmother's maiden name. I liked it. It had pizzazz.

My next favorite was my maternal grandmother's full name: Lily Diamond. Kind of reminded me of a stripper. And really, spewing forth about my bulimia certainly contained an element of stripping myself bare. I liked the allusion.

At the time I was stringing sentences together about saying "so long" to ED, my mother was eighty-seven and showing absolutely no signs of memory loss, Alzheimer's or dementia. Publishing anonymously would circumvent the problem of confessing to my mother the sordid details of my eating disorder, since the soundness of her mind seemed to be stable. What kind of a monster wishes dementia on a parent? I am not going to answer that.

Publishing anonymously would save my adult children from embarrassment and my grandchildren from potential playground ridicule. Or was I just so over-thinking this? The book would probably make no discernible splash and my agonizing would all be for naught.

So I reluctantly discarded the notion of publishing without using my real name.

First of all, I wanted to own my addiction. How else could I be a credible advocate if I was still carrying the mantle of shame along with me? I was proud of myself for overcoming and squashing ED. I was proud of myself for re-learning how to eat healthily and to handle my demons in a more constructive manner. Why hide it?

Second of all, from a purely practical side, how could I publicly speak about severing my relationship with ED if I were anonymous? I couldn't exactly show up at conferences and workshops, on TV and on YouTube with a bag over my head. What kind of marketing blitz could I hope to launch, hampered with a hidden identity?

The other complication was my slice-of-life column that I had been writing for years. My best friend Gloria warned me that using my column to broach the subject of my eating disorder—using it as a kick-off—could backfire. "People would be disappointed and disillusioned," she warned me. "For so long they viewed you as a coper extraordinaire."

It was tempting to block out the whole threatening situation. And as the days passed and the words flowed, I did. And so my mantra became: I will deal with it when the opportunity presents itself and when I have to.

But a quote by Maya Angelou kept nagging at me. "We delight in the beauty of the butterfly, but rarely admit the changes it has gone through to achieve that beauty."

It was an observation worthy of pondering. And for many days during the laborious writing of this manuscript, that is what I did. And in the process, I came to cherish the changes I went through and became eager to share the process, using my own name.

Months Pass

Months pass. Soon it will be almost 2,000 days since I have gone into my first floor powder room, closed the door and locked it, planted both feet firmly on the floor facing the commode and proceeded to puke my guts out.

What's changed?

No more eating the same thing every day out of habit and fear. I now ask myself before each meal: What do I feel like eating? Is it something salty? Spicy? Sweet? Laced with protein? Saturated with carbs? Light and airy? Fresh and dewy? Mindfully, I then make my choices.

I now ask myself before each meal: How much will it take to experience satiety—that warm bubble in my tummy that expands enough to stem the hunger but not enough to uncomfortably tighten the waistband of my jeans?

No more anxiously perusing an unfamiliar menu when dining out—automatically seeking out the least fattening menu item—in my vigilant effort to keep the needle on the scale from traveling north.

Now I am more mindful of what tickles my senses. And I am indulging in my desires.

It's working. My weight is stable. My blood work is perfectly normal. And I am finding pleasure in food rather than viewing sustenance as a whirlwind force constantly begging for restraint and corralling.

Quirks

Okay, so I've still got a few quirks.

I still get a pit in my stomach the night before I go for my monthly weigh-in at Weight Watchers.

And I don't eat anything the morning that I get weighed.

And I void my bladder before I step on the scale.

And if no one else is around, but me and the weigh-in lady, I have been known not only to slip off my oversized watch, but my skirt too, in order to stay within goal range.

I wear the same exact outfit each time—to minimize arbitrary weight fluctuations.

I take my first cup of morning coffee with me in the car, but no sips until after weigh-in.

I go with trepidation, sometimes dread, and usually outright anxiety. But I go.

My weight is stable and the brown skirt with the white polka dots fits comfortably.

I enjoy eating.

I enjoy searching out new recipes.

I enjoy trying new foods.

I even enjoy going to celebrations where food indulgence is front and center.

I enjoy drinking a glass of white wine and digging into pecan pie for dessert.

And every day, I pat myself on the back for beating ED to a pulp and reclaiming my power.

Opening Up the Umbrella

This is my story.

I hope the steps I took to get and stay ED-less will inspire, motivate and help you and the ones you love who face the same (or different) demons. I hope it will lend momentum to the arduous, but ultimately self-satisfying, journey of moving from disease toward health, balance and restoration. I hope my shared saga provides comfort. I hope it inspires you to act to bring about a healthy resolution to the demons tormenting you.

I released myself from the tired, misconceived mantra that I could get rid of ED by myself. Paradoxically, I realized I had the life skills to tackle ED but I needed a team to help me accomplish it and reach the goal line.

Seeking help enabled me to become my own agent for change. To stop attacking my body. To take stock of all the strengths I had acquired over the years and had always underestimated. To shed the idea that I needed ED by my side in order to be in control, in order to cope, in order to soar.

Reach for a state of positive equilibrium.

Unyoke the harness and break free of the chains.

Life's too short and too precious to slog along in the mist.

Open your umbrella and sing in the rain.

Action Steps for Recovery

- Admit you are an out-of-control bulimic.
- Allow yourself to feel the fear. When the fear of harming yourself becomes greater than the comfort bingeing and purging provides, movement away from disordered eating occurs.
- Avoid Internet intimacy with sites that espouse pro-bulimia behavior.
- Confide in someone you trust that you are bulimic.
- Seek out humor to raise your spirits and dispel the darkness.
- Recognize and record binge triggers.
- Hope is not a plan. Hope is fuel that propels the plan. Implement a plan. Cultivate hope.
- Implement ONE rule: No purging. No matter how much you eat.
- Step out of your comfort zone and find a therapist/eating disorder treatment center. If that's not working for you, find another.
- Allow others to care for you—resisting the urge to mother others in your group at your own expense.
- Explore your most intimate relationships. How are they helping or hindering your healing process? Learn how you can utilize their love and support to propel you toward greater emotional and physical well-being.

- Communicate what you need.
- Re-tool, refine and perfect your anger and anxiety management skills.
- Resist the pull that lulls you into thinking that a little initial success means you can overcome bulimia without professional help and guidance.
- Recognize the strongly ingrained cultural bias toward beauty/thinness/youth. Your attitude toward your body can change, although society's probably won't.
- Accept your proclivity to fear the scale—and carry on in spite of it.
- Develop a "Who Ya Gonna Call" list and use it.
- Unearth ten enjoyable activities and start doing them.
- Revel in the mouse-bites of progress. Small steps are sustainable steps.
- Chant: IBICBB. IBICBB. IBICBB. (I believe I can beat bulimia.)
- If you have an opportunity to experience Art Therapy, by all means PLEASE embrace it. It's a window into your inner world.
- Your story: Own it. Tell it.
- Explore the meaning of your dreams.
- Heed HALT: *h*unger, *a*nger, *l*oneliness, *t*iredness.
- You can't get around it. You must embrace the concept of Intuitive Eating. Read about it. Think about it. Practice it. Internalize it. Practice it. And practice it some more. It's a gradual transformation.
- Employ a willingness to forge new paths and habits.
- Ask for what you NEED. Articulate what you FEEL.
- Indulge in: A little shopping, honey. A little frivolity, dearie. A little escapism—TV binge watching (not eating) works wonders, lovey.

From the Author

Why did I write this book? How do I think my book will help? There is nothing else like it out there. It's not as detailed as a professional writing a how-to. It's not as agonizingly spewed forth as an eating disordered addict shedding her baggage. I write whimsically. No rigid guidelines, no exhaustive to-do lists. *The Secret Life of a Weight-Obsessed Woman* is the story of my forty-six-year journey with ED as a constant companion—as a source of both comfort and repulsion.

I want my book to simply, honestly and forthrightly reflect my struggles and my triumphs—to provide inspiration to others who think they cannot beat their own ED to a pulp. Because I believe they can.

The comments from my friends have led me to believe that too many women don't really know the intricacies of what an eating disorder is, how it impacts everyday life and both minor and major decisions—how ED insidiously creeps into all facets of one's being. The overall reaction from my close friends when I confessed that I was bulimic was, "I had no idea." They had no idea I was bulimic and they had no idea of what having an eating disorder really encompassed. So perhaps this book can also help people who know someone they suspect is bulimic—better understand their everyday struggles, their bizarre eating patterns, their strange attitudes about food and meals and snacks and desserts. Maybe my story will even propel them to muster up the courage to approach the family member, friend, neighbor or co-worker.

I made light of my burden. I kept everyone out of the loop. To even those few who knew—my husband, sister and one or two friends—I made it clear that the subject of my bulimia was off limits. Even when I went for couples therapy or individual therapy, I didn't deal with it—especially in those early years before what I was doing even had a name. I discussed my anxieties, my frustrations, my incessant time limitations, my depression and my anger. But not my bulimia. I truly believed it was not something I could ever overcome. And that if I could fix the other "stuff" in my life, I could keep ED safely in his silo—with minimal collateral damage.

I made light of the toxicity.

I minimized the deadliness.

I refused to register the seriousness.

I felt it was my burden to bear. Alone.

And though I unabashedly confided to friends about the ever-changing state of my marriage, my job particulars, my professional goals and challenges, and my parenting dilemmas, my bulimia was not something I discussed with them either. Ever.

What did I fear? I felt that if I couldn't tame the raging monster within, I'd lose the love and comfort of the people most important in my life. Sadly, if I had been convinced that my closest support system would stick with me whether I beat ED or not, I think I would have shed the secret earlier and with less anguish. This is not a criticism of my inner circle, it's more a reflection of a deep-seated, faulty assumption that if I wasn't perfect, I wasn't worthy of love.

Johann Hari, author of *Chasing the Scream: The First and Last Days of the War on Drugs*, said an addict who won't stop shouldn't be shunned. In a Huffington Post blog on January 20, 2015, he wrote, "that will only deepen their addiction—and you may lose them altogether."

So many of us have an "ED" in our lives. Call it an Existential Demon. Ever-present Demon. Emergent Demon. Emotional Demon. Encumbering Demon. Endless Demon. Entrenched Demon. Entangled Demon. Episodic Demon. Exhausting Demon.

Our own personal demon can stem from compulsive behaviors like gambling, shopping incessantly, over-exercising, drinking to excess, working round the clock, zoning out on social media, binge eating, and/or restricted eating. We inject, imbibe, shovel in, cut, snort, spend, and wager—in excess—in an attempt to make sense of our own jumbled narrative.

And loving us—not cutting us off—is what we need most. Embrace us. Help us. Stick with us. And we will try our damnedest not to disappoint you.

Postscript

Early 2017

I believe people appear in your life when you are ready to receive their wisdom.

I'm busy wrapping up my manuscript on bulimia. But I'm still grappling with my thinking that my bulimia was a long-ingrained habit that I was able to break. Something about that doesn't ring true. Something about that makes me uncomfortable. It's too dismissive. It's too simplistic. It's just not right.

Dr. Nina Savelle-Rocklin is a Los Angeles-based psychoanalyst who specializes in weight, food and body image issues. She contacted me after reading my nine-part Huffington Post series on my battle with bulimia. And at the end of 2016, she sent me an advance copy of her book, *Food for Thought—Perspectives on Eating Disorders*.

Honestly, for some unknown reason, I resisted reading her book for days, until one night the familiar stirrings of insatiable physical hunger began creeping over me. And the urge to rip open the box of Oreos in my pantry shouted out at me.

I knew I was tired. I knew I was missing my grandkids. And I knew I was overwhelmed with too many details and too little time to attend to them. Not a wholly unusual state of mind for me. So, where was this voracious hunger stemming from? What the hell was going on? I had broken my binge/purge "habit" almost five years ago. Habits that are broken just don't miraculously re-appear.

Furiously, I flipped through the pages of *Food for Thought*.

The following paragraph jumped off the page at me: "Many patients report that bulimia started as a seemingly magical solution to overeating or bingeing. They got rid of what they had eaten by vomiting, fasting or over-exercising ...They believe bulimia is a habit that they are unable or unwilling to break. The reality is that bulimia is a far more complicated condition than a deleterious habit. Bulimia is a symptom that contains and expresses a plethora of meanings; it can be understood as a defense against painful emotional experience, an expression of ambivalence, an attempt at mastery, and a means of self-regulation."

Wow. What a provocative, mind-blowing paragraph!

The very next morning I brewed myself a strong cup of coffee, ensconced myself in my wicker rocker on my back porch, took a deep breath, and delved deeper into Nina's treatise on the deep-seated causes of bulimia.

Here are a few interesting tidbits on the unresolved issues of a bulimic, gleaned from my reading:

- An unfulfilled wish for comfort and connection
- A turning against unmet needs
- Yearnings that lead to humiliation
- A disguising of internal conflicts
- A use of the body as the rage
- A control over unwanted urges
- An unrecognized strategy to clean up internal messiness

Breakthrough!!!!!!

These were all issues I had been working on—both in and out of therapy—for years. My ability to break the disordered eating cycle was based on my having come to terms with my inner turmoil. I had learned to honor the untidiness of my emotions, manage my anger, and accept my imperfections. I had practiced embracing the people I loved so passionately, with less fear and more realistic expectations. I had trained myself to tolerate criticism and welcome honest feedback. And through my writing and my speaking, I had channeled my angst into self-healing words and actions that dispelled so many faulty assumptions I had carried around for far too long. And all this allowed me to break through my self-imposed isolation, becoming re-engaged and re-vitalized.

By my own choosing, the topic of my bulimia was never explored in therapy. The irony: the thorny issues that made my eating disorder so pervasive in my life were the very issues that I had worked on every day of my life.

And why is this so freeing and why am I choosing to end my book with this postscript?

Because you may be closer than you think to eradicating your demons.

Because unbeknownst to you, the reasons for the existence of your demons may not be as compelling as they were when they first took hold.

Because your life skills and your mastery over your untidy and un-resolved emotions may be far more developed than you give yourself credit for.

Let me know.

I care.

Iris Ruth Pastor
irisruthpastor@gmail.com

Acknowledgments

Writing a book on my forty-six year relationship with ED (eating disorder) was not easy. And certainly was not a one-woman show.

I give immense credit to my team of professionals for their support and guidance: Editing—Diane Krause and Paula Stahel. Social Media—David Blacker and Ajla Subasic of Venerated Digital and Dan Blank of We Grow Media. Smith Publicity. Cover designer— Robin Brooks.

Helping birth this baby were many whose feedback I cherish and heeded: Deb Ochstein, Jean Peck, Stacey Cahn-Shapiro, Bette Strauss, Michele Bass, Hope Barnett, Hal Levine, Bev Richman, Gloria Peerless, Rebecca Hearst, Naomi Frankel, Linda Weinroth, Tawny McCormick, nieces Courtney and Suzanne, and my sister Lori Luckman. (Please forgive me if I left someone out—the fault lies with my aging genes.)

Thank you to my five sons and three daughters-in-law who never once looked over my shoulder to scrutinize what I was writing. To my husband, who in spite of airing some really personal stuff, still happily wakes up beside me every morning. And to my mother, for not freaking out when my story went public.

CPSIA information can be obtained
at www.ICGtesting.com
Printed in the USA
LVHW09s2351181018
594105LV00001B/100/P

9 780965 283236